UNITED
WE
STAND

A Message for All Americans

UNITED
WE
STAND

A Message for All Americans

Edited by J. W. Edwards and Louis DeRose

MUNDUS™

Published by Mundus™
A Registered Trademark of Ann Arbor Media Group, LLC
2500 S. State Street, Ann Arbor, MI 48104

Printed and bound in the United States of America
by Edwards Brothers, Inc.

ISBN 1-58726-020-4

10 9 8 7 6 5 4 3 2 1

Dedication

This book is dedicated to the victims of September 11, 2001.

America's Heroes

United Airlines Flight 175 (World Trade Center, South Tower)
American Airlines Flight 11 (World Trade Center, North Tower)
American Airlines Flight 77 (The Pentagon)
United Airlines Flight 93 (Shanksville, Pennsylvania)

World Trade Center, New York City, New York

The Pentagon, Arlington, Virginia

New York City Firefighters
New York City Police
Medical Personnel and Facilities
Clergy from all Faiths
American Red Cross
Rescue Workers
Tradesmen
U.S. Civil Servants
U.S. Military
Volunteers from across America

To Every United States Citizen
United We Stand

Contents

Statement by the President in His Address to the Nation

8:30 P.M. EDT
September 11, 2001

THE PRESIDENT: Good evening. Today, our fellow citizens, our way of life, our very freedom came under attack in a series of deliberate and deadly terrorist acts. The victims were in airplanes, or in their offices; secretaries, businessmen and women, military and federal workers; moms and dads, friends and neighbors. Thousands of lives were suddenly ended by evil, despicable acts of terror.

The pictures of airplanes flying into buildings, fires burning, huge structures collapsing, have filled us with disbelief, terrible sadness, and a quiet, unyielding anger. These acts of mass murder were intended to frighten our nation into chaos and retreat. But they have failed; our country is strong.

A great people has been moved to defend a great nation. Terrorist attacks can shake the foundations of our biggest buildings, but they cannot touch the foundation of America. These acts shattered steel, but they cannot dent the steel of American resolve.

America was targeted for attack because we're the brightest beacon for freedom and opportunity in the world. And no one will keep that light from shining.

Today, our nation saw evil, the very worst of human nature. And we responded with the best of America — with the daring of our rescue workers, with the caring for strangers and neighbors who came to give blood and help in any way they could.

Immediately following the first attack, I implemented our government's emergency response plans. Our military is powerful, and it's prepared. Our emergency teams are working in New York City and Washington, D.C. to help with local rescue efforts.

Our first priority is to get help to those who have been injured, and to take every precaution to protect our citizens at home and around the world from further attacks.

The functions of our government continue without interruption. Federal agencies in Washington which had to be evacuated today are reopening for essential personnel tonight, and will be open for business tomorrow. Our financial institutions remain strong, and the American economy will be open for business, as well.

The search is underway for those who are behind these evil acts. I've directed the full resources of our intelligence and law enforcement communities to find those responsible and to bring them to justice. We will make no distinction between the terrorists who committed these acts and those who harbor them.

I appreciate so very much the members of Congress who have joined me in strongly condemning these attacks. And on behalf of the American people, I thank the many world leaders who have called to offer their condolences and assistance.

America and our friends and allies join with all those who want peace and security in the world, and we stand together to win the war against terrorism. Tonight, I ask for your prayers for all those who grieve, for the children whose worlds have been shattered, for all whose sense of safety and security has been threatened. And I pray they will be comforted by a power greater than any of us, spoken through the ages in Psalm 23: "Even though I walk through the valley of the shadow of death, I fear no evil, for You are with me."

This is a day when all Americans from every walk of life unite in our resolve for justice and peace. America has stood down enemies before, and we will do so this time. None of us will ever forget this day. Yet, we go forward to defend freedom and all that is good and just in our world.

Thank you. Good night, and God bless America.

National Day of Prayer and Remembrance for the Victims of the Terrorist Attacks on September 11, 2001

By the President of the United States of America
A PROCLAMATION
September 13, 2001

On Tuesday morning, September 11, 2001, terrorists attacked America in a series of despicable acts of war. They hijacked four passenger jets, crashed two of them into the World Trade Center's twin towers and a third into the Headquarters of the U.S. Department of Defense at the Pentagon, causing great loss of life and tremendous damage. The fourth plane crashed in the Pennsylvania countryside, killing all on board but falling well short of its intended target apparently because of the heroic efforts of passengers on board. This carnage, which caused the collapse of both Trade Center towers and the destruction of part of the Pentagon, killed more than 250 airplane passengers and thousands more on the ground.

Civilized people around the world denounce the evildoers who devised and executed these terrible attacks. Justice demands that those who helped or harbored the terrorists be punished — and punished severely. The enormity of their evil demands it. We will use all the resources of the United States and our cooperating friends and allies to pursue those responsible for this evil, until justice is done.

We mourn with those who have suffered great and disastrous loss. All our hearts have been seared by the sudden and sense-less taking of innocent lives. We pray for healing and for the strength to serve and encourage one another in hope and faith.

Scripture says: "Blessed are those who mourn for they shall be comforted." I call on every American family and the family of America to observe a National Day of Prayer and Remembrance, honoring the memory of the thousands of victims of these brutal attacks and comforting those who lost loved ones. We will persevere through this national tragedy and personal loss. In time, we will find healing and recovery; and, in the face of all this evil, we remain strong and united, "one Nation under God."

NOW, THEREFORE, I, GEORGE W. BUSH, President of the United States of America, by virtue of the authority vested in me by the Constitution and laws of the United States, do hereby proclaim Friday, September 14, 2001, as a National Day of Prayer and Remembrance for the Victims of the Terrorist Attacks on September 11, 2001. I ask that the people of the United States and places of worship mark this National Day of Prayer and Remembrance with noontime memorial services, the ringing of bells at that hour, and evening candlelight remembrance vigils. I encourage employers to permit their workers time off during the lunch hour to attend the noontime services to pray for our land. I invite the people of the world who share our grief to join us in these solemn observances.

IN WITNESS WHEREOF, I have hereunto set my hand this thirteenth day of September, in the year of our Lord two thousand one, and of the Independence of the United States of America the two hundred and twenty-sixth.

—GEORGE W. BUSH

President's Remarks at National Day of Prayer and Remembrance

The National Cathedral
Washington, D.C.
1:00 P.M. EDT
September 14, 2001

THE PRESIDENT: We are here in the middle hour of our grief. So many have suffered so great a loss, and today we express our nation's sorrow. We come before God to pray for the missing and the dead, and for those who love them.

On Tuesday, our country was attacked with deliberate and massive cruelty. We have seen the images of fire and ashes, and bent steel.

Now come the names, the list of casualties we are only beginning to read. They are the names of men and women who began their day at a desk or in an airport, busy with life. They are the names of people who faced death, and in their last moments called home to say, be brave, and I love you.

They are the names of passengers who defied their murderers, and prevented the murder of others on the ground. They are the names of men and women who wore the uniform of the United States, and died at their posts.

They are the names of rescuers, the ones whom death found running up the stairs and into the fires to help others. We will read all these names. We will linger over them, and learn their stories, and many Americans will weep.

To the children and parents and spouses and families and friends of the lost, we offer the deepest sympathy of the nation. And I assure you,

you are not alone.

Just three days removed from these events, Americans do not yet have the distance of history. But our responsibility to history is already clear: to answer these attacks and rid the world of evil.

War has been waged against us by stealth and deceit and murder. This nation is peaceful, but fierce when stirred to anger. This conflict was begun on the timing and terms of others. It will end in a way, and at an hour, of our choosing.

Our purpose as a nation is firm. Yet our wounds as a people are recent and unhealed, and lead us to pray. In many of our prayers this week, there is a searching, and an honesty. At St. Patrick's Cathedral in New York on Tuesday, a woman said, "I prayed to God to give us a sign that He is still here." Others have prayed for the same, searching hospital to hospital, carrying pictures of those still missing.

God's signs are not always the ones we look for. We learn in tragedy that his purposes are not always our own. Yet the prayers of private suffering, whether in our homes or in this great cathedral, are known and heard, and understood.

There are prayers that help us last through the day, or endure the night. There are prayers of friends and strangers, that give us strength for the journey. And there are prayers that yield our will to a will greater than our own.

This world He created is of moral design. Grief and tragedy and hatred are only for a time. Goodness, remembrance, and love have no end. And the Lord of life holds all who die, and all who mourn.

It is said that adversity introduces us to ourselves. This is true of a nation as well. In this trial, we have been reminded, and the world has seen, that our fellow Americans are generous and kind, resourceful and brave. We see our national character in rescuers working past exhaustion; in long lines of blood donors; in thousands of citizens who have asked to work and serve in any way possible.

And we have seen our national character in eloquent acts of sacrifice. Inside the World Trade Center, one man who could have saved himself stayed until the end at the side of his quadriplegic friend. A beloved priest died giving the last rites to a firefighter. Two office workers, finding a disabled stranger, carried her down sixty-eight floors to safety. A group of men drove through the night from Dallas to Washington to bring skin grafts for burn victims.

In these acts, and in many others, Americans showed a deep commitment to one another, and an abiding love for our country. Today, we feel what Franklin Roosevelt called the warm courage of national unity. This is a unity of every faith, and every background.

It has joined together political parties in both houses of Congress. It is evident in services of prayer and candlelight vigils, and American flags, which are displayed in pride, and wave in defiance.

Our unity is a kinship of grief, and a steadfast resolve to prevail against our enemies. And this unity against terror is now extending across the world.

America is a nation full of good fortune, with so much to be grateful for. But we are not spared from suffering. In every generation, the world has produced enemies of human freedom. They have attacked America, because we are freedom's home and defender. And the commitment of our fathers is now the calling of our time.

On this national day of prayer and remembrance, we ask almighty God to watch over our nation, and grant us patience and resolve in all that is to come. We pray that He will comfort and console those who now walk in sorrow. We thank Him for each life we now must mourn, and the promise of a life to come.

As we have been assured, neither death nor life, nor angels nor principalities nor powers, nor things present nor things to come, nor height nor depth, can separate us from God's love. May He bless the souls of the departed. May He comfort our own. And may He always guide our country.

God bless America.

Declaration of National Emergency by Reason of Certain Terrorist Attacks

By the President of the United States of America
A PROCLAMATION
September 14, 2001

A national emergency exists by reason of the terrorist attacks at the World Trade Center, New York, New York, and the Pentagon, and the continuing and immediate threat of further attacks on the United States.

NOW, THEREFORE, I, GEORGE W. BUSH, President of the United States of America, by virtue of the authority vested in me as President by the Constitution and the laws of the United States, I hereby declare that the national emergency has existed since September 11, 2001, and, pursuant to the National Emergencies Act (50 U.S.C. 1601 et seq.), I intend to utilize the following statutes: sections 123, 123a, 527, 2201(c), 12006, and 12302 of title 10, United States Code, and sections 331, 359, and 367 of title 14, United States Code.

This proclamation immediately shall be published in the Federal Register or disseminated through the Emergency Federal Register, and transmitted to the Congress.

This proclamation is not intended to create any right or benefit, substantive or procedural, enforceable at law by a party against the United States, its agencies, its officers, or any person.

IN WITNESS WHEREOF, I have hereunto set my hand this fourteenth day of September, in the year of our Lord two thousand one, and of the Independence of the United States of America the two hundred and twenty-sixth.

—GEORGE W. BUSH

President Extends Order for Flags at Half-Staff

AMENDING PROCLAMATION 7461
Display of the Flag at Half-Staff as a Mark of Respect
for the Victim of the Incidents on Tuesday, September 11, 2001

By the President of the United States of America
A PROCLAMATION

By the authority vested in me as President of the United States by the Constitution and the laws of the United States of America, and in order to extend the display of the flag at half-staff as a mark of respect for the victims of the terrorist attacks on Tuesday, September 11, 2001, it is hereby ordered that Proclamation 7461 of September 11, 2001, is amended by deleting in the first sentence the words "Sunday, September 16" and inserting in their place the words "Saturday, September 22."

IN WITNESS WHEREOF, I have hereunto set my hand this fourteenth day of September, in the year of our Lord two thousand one, and of the Independence of the United States of America the two hundred and twenty-sixth.

—GEORGE W. BUSH

Address to a Joint Session of Congress and the American People

United States Capitol, Washington, D.C.
9:00 P.M. EDT
September 20, 2001

THE PRESIDENT: Mr. Speaker, Mr. President Pro Tempore, members of Congress, and fellow Americans:

In the normal course of events, Presidents come to this chamber to report on the state of the Union. Tonight, no such report is needed. It has already been delivered by the American people.

We have seen it in the courage of passengers, who rushed terrorists to save others on the ground – passengers like an exceptional man named Todd Beamer. And would you please help me to welcome his wife, Lisa Beamer, here tonight.

We have seen the state of our Union in the endurance of rescuers, working past exhaustion. We have seen the unfurling of flags, the lighting of candles, the giving of blood, the saying of prayers – in English, Hebrew, and Arabic. We have seen the decency of a loving and giving people who have made the grief of strangers their own.

My fellow citizens, for the last nine days, the entire world has seen for itself the state of our Union – and it is strong.

Tonight we are a country awakened to danger and called to defend freedom. Our grief has turned to anger, and anger to resolution. Whether we bring our enemies to justice, or bring justice to our enemies, justice will be done.

I thank the Congress for its leadership at such an important time. All of America was touched on the evening of the tragedy to see Republicans and Democrats joined together on the steps of this Capitol, singing "God Bless America." And you did more than sing; you acted, by delivering $40 billion to rebuild our communities and meet the needs of our military. Speaker Hastert, Minority Leader Gephardt, Majority Leader Daschle and Senator Lott, I thank you for your friendship, for your leadership and for your service to our country.

And on behalf of the American people, I thank the world for its out-pouring of support. America will never forget the sounds of our National Anthem playing at Buckingham Palace, on the streets of Paris, and at Berlin's Brandenburg Gate.

We will not forget South Korean children gathering to pray outside our embassy in Seoul, or the prayers of sympathy offered at a mosque in Cairo. We will not forget moments of silence and days of mourning in Australia and Africa and Latin America.

Nor will we forget the citizens of 80 other nations who died with our own: dozens of Pakistanis; more than 130 Israelis; more than 250 citizens of India; men and women from El Salvador, Iran, Mexico and Japan; and hundreds of British citizens. America has no truer friend than Great Britain. Once again, we are joined together in a great cause – so honored the British Prime Minister has crossed an ocean to show his unity of purpose with America. Thank you for coming, friend.

On September the 11th, enemies of freedom committed an act of war against our country. Americans have known wars – but for the past 136 years, they have been wars on foreign soil, except for one Sunday in 1941. Americans have known the casualties of war – but not at the center of a great city on a peaceful morning. Americans have known surprise attacks – but never before on thousands of civilians. All of this was brought upon us in a single day – and night fell on a different world, a world where freedom itself is under attack.

Americans have many questions tonight. Americans are asking: Who attacked our country? The evidence we have gathered all points to a collection of loosely affiliated terrorist organizations known as al Qaeda. They are the same murderers indicted for bombing American embassies in Tanzania and Kenya, and responsible for bombing the USS Cole.

Al Qaeda is to terror what the mafia is to crime. But its goal is not making money; its goal is remaking the world – and imposing its radical beliefs on people everywhere.

The terrorists practice a fringe form of Islamic extremism that has been rejected by Muslim scholars and the vast majority of Muslim clerics – a fringe movement that perverts the peaceful teachings of Islam. The terrorists' directive commands them to kill Christians and Jews, to kill all Americans, and make no distinction among military and civilians, including women and children.

This group and its leader – a person named Osama bin Laden – are linked to many other organizations in different countries, including the Egyptian Islamic Jihad and the Islamic Movement of Uzbekistan. There are thousands of these terrorists in more than 60 countries. They are recruited from their own nations and neighborhoods and brought to camps in places like Afghanistan, where they are trained in the tactics of terror. They are sent back to their homes or sent to hide in countries around the world to plot evil and destruction.

The leadership of al Qaeda has great influence in Afghanistan and supports the Taliban regime in controlling most of that country. In Afghanistan, we see al Qaeda's vision for the world.

Afghanistan's people have been brutalized – many are starving and many have fled. Women are not allowed to attend school. You can be jailed for owning a television. Religion can be practiced only as their leaders dictate. A man can be jailed in Afghanistan if his beard is not long enough.

The United States respects the people of Afghanistan – after all, we are currently its largest source of humanitarian aid – but we condemn the Taliban regime. It is not only repressing its own people, it is threatening people everywhere by sponsoring and sheltering and supplying terrorists. By aiding and abetting murder, the Taliban regime is committing murder.

And tonight, the United States of America makes the following demands on the Taliban: Deliver to United States authorities all the leaders of al Qaeda who hide in your land. Release all foreign nationals, including American citizens, you have unjustly imprisoned. Protect foreign journalists, diplomats and aid workers in your country. Close immediately and permanently every terrorist training camp in Afghanistan, and hand over every terrorist, and every person in their support structure, to appropriate authorities. Give the United States full access to terrorist training camps, so we can make sure they are no longer operating.

These demands are not open to negotiation or discussion. The Taliban must act, and act immediately. They will hand over the terrorists, or they will share in their fate.

I also want to speak tonight directly to Muslims throughout the world. We respect your faith. It's practiced freely by many millions of Americans, and by millions more in countries that America counts as friends. Its teachings are good and peaceful, and those who commit evil in the name of Allah blaspheme the name of Allah. The terrorists are traitors to their own faith, trying, in effect, to hijack Islam itself. The enemy of America is not our many Muslim friends; it is not our many Arab friends. Our enemy is a radical network of terrorists, and every government that supports them.

Our war on terror begins with al Qaeda, but it does not end there. It will not end until every terrorist group of global reach has been found, stopped and defeated.

Americans are asking, why do they hate us? They hate what we see right here in this chamber – a democratically elected government. Their leaders are self-appointed. They hate our freedoms – our freedom of religion, our freedom of speech, our freedom to vote and assemble and disagree with each other.

They want to overthrow existing governments in many Muslim countries, such as Egypt, Saudi Arabia, and Jordan. They want to drive Israel out of the Middle East. They want to drive Christians and Jews out of vast regions of Asia and Africa.

These terrorists kill not merely to end lives, but to disrupt and end a way of life. With every atrocity, they hope that America grows fearful, retreating from the world and forsaking our friends. They stand against us, because we stand in their way.

We are not deceived by their pretenses to piety. We have seen their kind before. They are the heirs of all the murderous ideologies of the 20th century. By sacrificing human life to serve their radical visions – by abandoning every value except the will to power – they follow in the path of fascism, and Nazism, and totalitarianism. And they will follow that path all the way, to where it ends: in history's unmarked grave of discarded lies.

Americans are asking: How will we fight and win this war? We will direct every resource at our command – every means of diplomacy, every tool of intelligence, every instrument of law enforcement, every financial influence, and every necessary weapon of war – to the disruption and to the defeat of the global terror network.

This war will not be like the war against Iraq a decade ago, with a decisive liberation of territory and a swift conclusion. It will not look like the air war above Kosovo two years ago, where no ground troops were used and not a single American was lost in combat.

Our response involves far more than instant retaliation and isolated strikes. Americans should not expect one battle, but a lengthy campaign, unlike any other we have ever seen. It may include dramatic strikes, visible on TV, and covert operations, secret even in success. We will starve terrorists of funding, turn them one against another, drive them from place to place, until there is no refuge or no rest. And we will pursue nations that provide aid or safe haven to terrorism. Every nation, in every region, now has a decision to make. Either you are with us, or you are with the terrorists. From this day forward, any nation that continues to harbor or support terrorism will be regarded by the United States as a hostile regime.

Our nation has been put on notice: We are not immune from attack. We will take defensive measures against terrorism to protect Americans. Today, dozens of federal departments and agencies, as well as state and local governments, have responsibilities affecting homeland security. These efforts must be coordinated at the highest level. So tonight I announce the creation of a Cabinet-level position reporting directly to me – the Office of Homeland Security.

And tonight I also announce a distinguished American to lead this effort, to strengthen American security: a military veteran, an effective governor, a true patriot, a trusted friend – Pennsylvania's Tom Ridge. He will lead, oversee and coordinate a comprehensive national strategy to safeguard our country against terrorism, and respond to any attacks that may come.

These measures are essential. But the only way to defeat terrorism as a threat to our way of life is to stop it, eliminate it, and destroy it where it grows.

Many will be involved in this effort, from FBI agents to intelligence operatives to the reservists we have called to active duty. All deserve our thanks, and all have our prayers. And tonight, a few miles from the damaged Pentagon, I have a message for our military: Be ready. I've called the Armed Forces to alert, and there is a reason. The hour is coming when America will act, and you will make us proud.

This is not, however, just America's fight. And what is at stake is not just America's freedom. This is the world's fight. This is civilization's fight. This is the fight of all who believe in progress and pluralism, tolerance and freedom.

We ask every nation to join us. We will ask, and we will need, the help of police forces, intelligence services, and banking systems around the world. The United States is grateful that many nations and many international organizations have already responded – with sympathy and with support. Nations from Latin America, to Asia, to Africa, to Europe, to the Islamic world. Perhaps the NATO Charter reflects best the attitude of the world: An attack on one is an attack on all.

The civilized world is rallying to America's side. They understand that if this terror goes unpunished, their own cities, their own citizens may be next. Terror, unanswered, can not only bring down buildings, it can threaten the stability of legitimate governments. And you know what – we're not going to allow it.

Americans are asking: What is expected of us? I ask you to live your lives, and hug your children. I know many citizens have fears tonight, and I ask you to be calm and resolute, even in the face of a continuing threat. I ask you to uphold the values of America, and remember why so many have come here. We are in a fight for our principles, and our first responsibility is to live by them. No one should be singled out for unfair treatment or unkind words because of their ethnic background or religious faith.

I ask you to continue to support the victims of this tragedy with your contributions. Those who want to give can go to a central source of information, libertyunites.org, to find the names of groups providing direct help in New York, Pennsylvania, and Virginia.

The thousands of FBI agents who are now at work in this investigation may need your cooperation, and I ask you to give it.

I ask for your patience, with the delays and inconveniences that may accompany tighter security; and for your patience in what will be a long struggle.

I ask your continued participation and confidence in the American economy. Terrorists attacked a symbol of American prosperity. They did not touch its source. America is successful because of the hard work, and creativity, and enterprise of our people. These were the true strengths of our economy before September 11th, and they are our strengths today.

And, finally, please continue praying for the victims of terror and their families, for those in uniform, and for our great country. Prayer has comforted us in sorrow, and will help strengthen us for the journey ahead.

Tonight I thank my fellow Americans for what you have already done and for what you will do. And ladies and gentlemen of the Congress, I thank you, their representatives, for what you have already done and for what we will do together.

Tonight, we face new and sudden national challenges. We will come together to improve air safety, to dramatically expand the number of air marshals on domestic flights, and take new measures to prevent hijacking. We will come together to promote stability and keep our airlines flying, with direct assistance during this emergency.

We will come together to give law enforcement the additional tools it needs to track down terror here at home. We will come together to strengthen our intelligence capabilities to know the plans of terrorists before they act, and find them before they strike. We will come together to take active steps that strengthen America's economy, and put our people back to work.

Tonight we welcome two leaders who embody the extraordinary spirit of all New Yorkers: Governor George Pataki, and Mayor Rudolph Giuliani. As a symbol of America's resolve, my administration will work with Congress, and these two leaders, to show the world that we will rebuild New York City.

After all that has just passed – all the lives taken, and all the possibilities and hopes that died with them – it is natural to wonder if America's future is one of fear. Some speak of an age of terror. I know there are struggles ahead, and dangers to face. But this country will define our times, not be defined by them. As long as the United States of America is determined and strong, this will not be an age of terror; this will be an age of liberty, here and across the world.

Great harm has been done to us. We have suffered great loss. And in our grief and anger we have found our mission and our moment.

Freedom and fear are at war. The advance of human freedom – the great achievement of our time, and the great hope of every time – now depends on us. Our nation – this generation – will lift a dark threat of violence from our people and our future. We will rally the world to this cause by our efforts, by our courage. We will not tire, we will not falter, and we will not fail.

It is my hope that in the months and years ahead, life will return almost to normal. We'll go back to our lives and routines, and that is good. Even grief recedes with time and grace. But our resolve must not pass. Each of us will remember what happened that day, and to whom it happened. We'll remember the moment the news came – where we were and what we were doing. Some will remember an image of a fire, or a story of rescue. Some will carry memories of a face and a voice gone forever.

And I will carry this: It is the police shield of a man named George Howard, who died at the World Trade Center trying to save others. It was given to me by his mom, Arlene, as a proud memorial to her son. This is my reminder of lives that ended, and a task that does not end.

I will not forget this wound to our country or those who inflicted it. I will not yield; I will not rest; I will not relent in waging this struggle for freedom and security for the American people.

The course of this conflict is not known, yet its outcome is certain. Freedom and fear, justice and cruelty, have always been at war, and we know that God is not neutral between them.

Fellow citizens, we'll meet violence with patient justice – assured of the rightness of our cause, and confident of the victories to come. In all that lies before us, may God grant us wisdom, and may He watch over the United States of America.

Thank you.

Radio Address of the President to the Nation

September 29, 2001

THE PRESIDENT: Good morning. I want to report to you on the progress being made on many fronts in our war against terrorism. This is a different kind of war, which we will wage aggressively and methodically to disrupt and destroy terrorist activity.

In recent days, many members of our military have left their homes and families and begun moving into a place for missions to come. Thousands of Reservists have been called to active duty. Soldiers, sailors, airmen, Marines and Coast Guardmen are being deployed to points around the globe, ready to answer when their country calls. Our military families have accepted many hardships, and our nation is grateful for their willing service.

The men and women of the Armed Forces are united in their dedication to freedom and they will make us proud in the struggle against terrorism.

International cooperation is gaining momentum. This week, I met with the Prime Ministers of two of America's closest friends: Canada and Japan. Other countries, from Russia to Indonesia, are giving strong support as the war against terrorism moves forward. America is grateful to the nations that have cut off diplomatic ties with the Taliban regime in Afghanistan, which is sheltering terrorists.

The United States respects the people of Afghanistan and we are their largest provider of humanitarian aid. But we condemn the Taliban, and welcome the support of other nations in isolating that regime.

We have also launched a strike against the financial foundation of the global terror network. Our goal is to deny terrorists the money they need to carry our their plans. We began by identifying 27 terrorist organizations, terrorist leaders and foreign businesses and charities that support or front for terrorism.

We froze whatever assets they had here in the United States, and we blocked them from doing business with people, companies or banks in our country. Many governments and financial institutions around the world are joining in this effort to starve terrorists of funding.

This week I visited the headquarters at the FBI and the CIA. Their agents and analysts have been on the case around the clock, uncovering and pursuing the enemy. In the long campaign ahead, they will need our continued support, and every necessary tool to do their work.

I'm asking Congress for new law enforcement authority, to better track the communications of terrorists, and to detain suspected terrorists until the moment they are deported. I will also seek more funding and better technology for our country's intelligence community.

This week, we also took strong steps to improve security on planes and in airports, and to restore confidence in air travel. We're providing airlines with federal grants to make cockpits more secure through measures including fortified doors and stronger locks. And we're dramatically increasing the number of federal air marshals on our planes.

Americans will have the confidence of knowing that fully equipped officers of the law are flying with them in far greater numbers. I'm also working with Congress to put federal law enforcement in charge of all bag and passenger screening at our airports. Standards will be tougher and enforced by highly trained professionals who know exactly what they're looking for. To enhance safety immediately, I've asked governors to place National Guardsmen at security checkpoints in airports.

As all these actions make clear, our war on terror will be much broader than the battlefields and beachheads of the past. This war will be fought wherever terrorists hide, or run, or plan. Some victories will be won outside of public view, in tragedies avoided and threats eliminated. Other victories will be clear to all.

Our weapons are military and diplomatic, financial and legal. And in this struggle, our greatest advantages are the patience and resolve of the American people.

We did not seek this conflict, but we will win it. America will act deliberately and decisively, and the cause of freedom will prevail. Thank you for listening.

Presidential Address to the Nation: The Treaty Room

1:00 P.M. EDT
October 7, 2001

THE PRESIDENT: Good afternoon. On my orders, the United States military has begun strikes against al Qaeda terrorist training camps and military installations of the Taliban regime in Afghanistan. These carefully targeted actions are designed to disrupt the use of Afghanistan as a terrorist base of operations, and to attack the military capability of the Taliban regime.

We are joined in this operation by our staunch friend, Great Britain. Other close friends, including Canada, Australia, Germany and France, have pledged forces as the operation unfolds. More than 40 countries in the Middle East, Africa, Europe and across Asia have granted air transit or landing rights. Many more have shared intelligence. We are supported by the collective will of the world.

More than two weeks ago, I gave Taliban leaders a series of clear and specific demands: Close terrorist training camps; hand over leaders of the al Qaeda network; and return all foreign nationals, including American citizens, unjustly detained in your country. None of these demands were met. And now the Taliban will pay a price. By destroying camps and disrupting communications, we will make it more difficult for the terror network to train new recruits and coordinate their evil plans.

Initially, the terrorists may burrow deeper into caves and other entrenched hiding places. Our military action is also designed to clear the way for sustained, comprehensive and relentless operations to drive them out and bring them to justice.

At the same time, the oppressed people of Afghanistan will know the generosity of America and our allies. As we strike military targets, we'll also drop food, medicine and supplies to the starving and suffering men and women and children of Afghanistan.

The United States of America is a friend to the Afghan people, and we are the friends of almost a billion worldwide who practice the Islamic faith. The United States of America is an enemy of those who aid terrorists and of the barbaric criminals who profane a great religion by committing murder in its name.

This military action is a part of our campaign against terrorism, another front in a war that has already been joined through diplomacy, intelligence, the freezing of financial assets and the arrests of known terrorists by law enforcement agents in 38 countries. Given the nature and reach of our enemies, we will win this conflict by the patient accumulation of successes, by meeting a series of challenges with determination and will and purpose.

Today we focus on Afghanistan, but the battle is broader. Every nation has a choice to make. In this conflict, there is no neutral ground. If any government sponsors the outlaws and killers of innocents, they have become outlaws and murderers, themselves. And they will take that lonely path at their own peril.

I'm speaking to you today from the Treaty Room of the White House, a place where American Presidents have worked for peace. We're a peaceful nation. Yet, as we have learned, so suddenly and so tragically, there can be no peace in a world of sudden terror. In the face of today's new threat, the only way to pursue peace is to pursue those who threaten it.

We did not ask for this mission, but we will fulfill it. The name of today's military operation is Enduring Freedom. We defend not only our precious freedoms, but also the freedom of people everywhere to live and raise their children free from fear.

I know many Americans feel fear today. And our government is taking strong precautions. All law enforcement and intelligence agencies are working aggressively around America, around the world and around the clock. At my request, many governors have activated the National Guard to strengthen airport security. We have called up Reserves to reinforce our military capability and strengthen the protection of our homeland.

In the months ahead, our patience will be one of our strengths –
patience with the long waits that will result from tighter security; patience
and understanding that it will take time to achieve our goals; patience in
all the sacrifices that may come.

Today, those sacrifices are being made by members of our Armed
Forces who now defend us so far from home, and by their proud and wor-
ried families. A Commander-in-Chief sends America's sons and daughters into a battle in a foreign land only after the greatest care and a lot of
prayer. We ask a lot of those who wear our uniform. We ask them to leave
their loved ones, to travel great distances, to risk injury, even to be prepared to make the ultimate sacrifice of their lives. They are dedicated,
they are honorable; they represent the best of our country. And we are
grateful.

To all the men and women in our military – every sailor, every soldier,
every airman, every coastguardsman, every Marine – I say this: Your mission is defined; your objectives are clear; your goal is just. You have my
full confidence, and you will have every tool you need to carry out your
duty.

I recently received a touching letter that says a lot about the state of
America in these difficult times – a letter from a 4th-grade girl, with a
father in the military: "As much as I don't want my Dad to fight," she
wrote, "I'm willing to give him to you."

This is a precious gift, the greatest she could give. This young girl
knows what America is all about. Since September 11, an entire generation of young Americans has gained new understanding of the value of
freedom, and its cost in duty and in sacrifice.

The battle is now joined on many fronts. We will not waver; we will not
tire; we will not falter; and we will not fail. Peace and freedom will prevail.

Thank you. May God continue to bless America.

Summary of the President's Executive Order

The Office of Homeland Security & the Homeland Security Council
The Office of Homeland Security
Mission & Management
October 8, 2001

The President will establish the Office of Homeland Security that will be headed by the Assistant to the President for Homeland Security – Governor Tom Ridge.

The mission of the Office will be to develop and coordinate the implementation of a comprehensive national strategy to secure the United States from terrorist threats or attacks. The Office will coordinate the executive branch's efforts to detect, prepare for, prevent, protect against, respond to, and recover from terrorist attacks within the United States.

National Strategy The Office will work with executive departments and agencies, state and local governments, and private entities to ensure the adequacy of the national strategy for detecting, preparing for, preventing, protecting against, responding to, and recovering from terrorist threats or attacks within the United States and will periodically review and coordinate revisions to that strategy as necessary.

Detection The Office will identify priorities and coordinate efforts for collection and analysis of information within the United States regarding threats of terrorism against the United States and activities of terrorists or terrorist groups within the United States. The Office will also identify, in coordination with the Assistant to the President for National Security Affairs, priorities for collection of intelligence outside the United States regarding threats of terrorism within the United States. The Office will work with federal, state, and local agencies to:

• facilitate collection from state and local governments and private entities of information pertaining to terrorist threats or activities within the United States;

• coordinate and prioritize the requirements for foreign intelligence relating to terrorism within the United States of executive departments and agencies responsible for homeland security, and provide these requirements and priorities to the Director of Central Intelligence and other agencies responsible for collection of foreign intelligence;

• coordinate efforts to ensure that all executive departments and agencies that have intelligence collection responsibilities have sufficient technological capabilities and resources to collect intelligence and data relating to terrorist activities or possible terrorist acts within the United States, working with the Assistant to the President for National Security Affairs, as appropriate;

• coordinate development of monitoring protocols and equipment for use in detecting the release of biological, chemical, and radiological hazards; and

• ensure that, to the extent permitted by law, all appropriate and necessary intelligence and law enforcement information relating to homeland security is disseminated to and exchanged among appropriate executive departments and agencies responsible for homeland security and, where appropriate for reasons of homeland security, promote exchange of such information with and among state and local governments and private entities.

Preparedness The Office of Homeland Security will coordinate national efforts to prepare for and mitigate the consequences of terrorist threats or attacks within the United States. In performing this function, the Office will work with federal, state, and local agencies, and private entities to:

• review and assess the adequacy of the portions of all federal emergency response plans that pertain to terrorist threats or attacks within the United States;

• coordinate domestic exercises and simulations designed to assess and practice systems that would be called upon to respond to a terrorist threat or attack within the United States and coordinate programs and activities for training federal, state, and local employees who would be called upon to respond to such a threat or attack;

• coordinate national efforts to ensure public health preparedness for a terrorist attack, including reviewing vaccination policies and reviewing the adequacy of and, if necessary, increasing vaccine and pharmaceutical stockpiles and hospital capacity;

• coordinate federal assistance to state and local authorities and non-governmental organizations to prepare for and respond to terrorist threats or attacks within the United States;

• ensure that national preparedness programs and activities for terrorist threats or attacks are developed and are regularly evaluated under appropriate standards and that resources are allocated to improving and sustaining preparedness based on such evaluations; and

• ensure the readiness and coordinated deployment of federal response teams to respond to terrorist threats or attacks, working with the Assistant to the President for National Security Affairs, when appropriate.

Prevention The Office will coordinate efforts to prevent terrorist attacks within the United States. In performing this function, the Office shall work with federal, state, and local agencies, and private entities to:

• facilitate the exchange of information among such agencies relating to immigration and visa matters and shipments of cargo; and, working with the Assistant to the President for National Security Affairs, ensure coordination among such agencies to prevent the entry of terrorists and terrorist materials and supplies into the United States and facilitate removal of such terrorists from the United States, when appropriate;

• coordinate efforts to investigate terrorist threats and attacks within the United States; and

• coordinate efforts to improve the security of United States borders, territorial waters, and airspace in order to prevent acts of terrorism within the United States, working with the Assistant to the President for National Security Affairs, when appropriate.

Protection The Office will coordinate efforts to protect the United States and its critical infrastructure from the consequences of terrorist attacks. In performing this function, the Office shall work with federal, state, and local agencies, and private entities to:

• strengthen measures for protecting energy production, transmission, and distribution services and critical facilities; other utilities; telecommunications; facilities that produce, use, store, or dispose of nuclear material; and other critical infrastructure services and critical facilities within the United States from terrorist attack;

• coordinate efforts to protect critical public and privately owned information systems within the United States from terrorist attack;

• develop criteria for reviewing whether appropriate security measures are in place at major public and privately owned facilities within the United States;

• coordinate domestic efforts to ensure that special events determined by appropriate senior officials to have national significance are protected from terrorist attack;

• coordinate efforts to protect transportation systems within the United States, including railways, highways, shipping, ports and waterways, and airports and civilian aircraft, from terrorist attack;

• coordinate efforts to protect United States livestock, agriculture, and systems for the provision of water and food for human use and consumption from terrorist attack; and

• coordinate efforts to prevent unauthorized access to, development of, and unlawful importation into the United States of, chemical, biological, radiological, nuclear, explosive, or other related materials that have the potential to be used in terrorist attacks.

Response and Recovery The Office will coordinate efforts to respond to and promote recovery from terrorist threats or attacks within the United States. In performing this function, the Office shall work with federal, state, and local agencies, and private entities to:

• coordinate efforts to ensure rapid restoration of transportation systems, energy production, transmission, and distribution systems; telecommunications; other utilities; and other critical infrastructure facilities after disruption by a terrorist threat or attack;

• coordinate efforts to ensure rapid restoration of public and private critical information systems after disruption by a terrorist threat or attack;

• work with the National Economic Council to coordinate efforts to stabilize United States financial markets after a terrorist threat or attack and manage the immediate economic and financial consequences of the incident;

• coordinate federal plans and programs to provide medical, financial, and other assistance to victims of terrorist attacks and their families; and

• coordinate containment and removal of biological, chemical, radiological, explosive, or other hazardous materials in the event of a terrorist threat or attack involving such hazards and coordinate efforts to mitigate the effects of such an attack.

Incident Management The Assistant to the President for Homeland Security will be the individual primarily responsible for coordinating the domestic response efforts of all departments and agencies in the event of an imminent terrorist threat and during and in the immediate aftermath of a terrorist attack within the United States and shall be the principal point of contact for and to the President with respect to coordination of such efforts. The Assistant to the President for Homeland Security will coordinate with the Assistant to the President for National Security Affairs, as appropriate.

Continuity of Government The Assistant to the President for Homeland Security, in coordination with the Assistant to the President for National Security Affairs, will review plans and preparations for ensuring the continuity of the Federal Government in the event of a terrorist attack that threatens the safety and security of the United States Government or its leadership.

Public Affairs The Office, subject to the direction of the White House Office of Communications, shall coordinate the strategy of the executive branch for communicating with the public in the event of a terrorist threat or attack within the United States. The Office also will coordinate the development of programs for educating the public about the nature of terrorist threats and appropriate precautions and responses.

Review of Legal Authorities and Development of Legislative Proposals The Office will coordinate a periodic review and assessment of the legal authorities available to executive departments and agencies to permit them to perform the functions described in this order. When the Office determines that such legal authorities are inadequate, the Office will develop, in consultation with executive departments and agencies, proposals for presidential action and legislative proposals for submission to the Office of Management and Budget to enhance the ability of executive departments and agencies to perform those functions. The Office will work with state and local governments in assessing the adequacy of their legal authorities to permit them to detect, prepare for, prevent, protect against, and recover from terrorist threats and attacks.

Budget Review The Assistant to the President for Homeland Security, in consultation with the Director of the Office of Management and Budget and the heads of executive departments and agencies, will identify programs that contribute to the Administration's strategy for homeland security and, in the development of the President's annual budget submission, shall review and provide advice to the heads of departments and agencies for such programs. The Assistant to the President for Homeland Security will provide advice to the Director on the level and use of funding in departments and agencies for homeland security-related activities and, prior to the Director's forwarding of the proposed annual budget submission to the President for transmittal to Congress, will certify to the Director the funding levels that the Assistant to the President for Homeland Security believes are necessary and appropriate for the homeland security-related activities of the executive branch.

Administration The Office of Homeland Security will be directed by the Assistant to the President for Homeland Security. The Office of Administration within the Executive Office of the President shall provide the Office of Homeland Security with such personnel, funding, and administrative support, to the extent permitted by law and subject to the availability of appropriations, as directed by the Chief of Staff to carry out the provisions of this order.

Heads of executive departments and agencies are authorized, to the extent permitted by law, to detail or assign personnel of such departments and agencies to the Office of Homeland Security upon request of the Assistant to the President for Homeland Security, subject to the approval of the Chief of Staff.

The Homeland Security Council The President's Executive Order establishes a Homeland Security Council which will be responsible for advising and assisting the President with respect to all aspects of homeland security. The Council will serve as the mechanism for ensuring coordination of homeland security-related activities of executive departments and agencies and effective development and implementation of homeland security policies.

The Council will have as its members the President, the Vice President, the Secretary of the Treasury, the Secretary of Defense, the Attorney

General, the Secretary of Health and Human Services, the Secretary of Transportation, the Director of the Federal Emergency Management Agency, the Director of the Federal Bureau of Investigation, the Director of Central Intelligence, the Assistant to the President for Homeland Security, and such other officers of the executive branch as the President may from time to time designate. The Chief of Staff, the Chief of Staff to the Vice President, the Assistant to the President for National Security Affairs, the Counsel to the President, and the Director of the Office of Management and Budget also are invited to attend any Council meeting. The Secretary of State, the Secretary of Agriculture, the Secretary of the Interior, the Secretary of Energy, the Secretary of Labor, the Secretary of Commerce, the Secretary of Veterans Affairs, the Administrator of the Environmental Protection Agency, the Assistant to the President for Economic Policy, and the Assistant to the President for Domestic Policy shall be invited to attend meetings pertaining to their responsibilities. The heads of other executive departments and agencies and other senior officials shall be invited to attend Council meetings when appropriate.

The Council will meet at the President's direction. When the President is absent from a meeting of the Council, at the President's direction the Vice President may preside. The Assistant to the President for Homeland Security will be responsible, at the President's direction, for determining the agenda, ensuring that necessary papers are prepared, and recording Council actions and Presidential decisions.

President Bush's Cabinet

The tradition of the Cabinet dates back to the beginnings of the Presidency itself. One of the principal purposes of the Cabinet (drawn from Article II, Section 2 of the Constitution) is to advise the President on any subject he may require relating to the duties of their respective offices.

The Cabinet includes the Vice President and, by law, the heads of 14 executive departments-the Secretaries of Agriculture, Commerce, Defense, Education, Energy, Health and Human Services, Housing and Urban Development, Interior, Labor, State, Transportation, Treasury, and Veterans Affairs, and the Attorney General. Under President George W. Bush, Cabinet-level rank also has been accorded to the Administrator, Environmental Protection Agency; Director, Office of Management and Budget; the Director, National Drug Control Policy; and the U.S. Trade Representative.

Secretary of Agriculture, Ann M. Veneman
Secretary of Commerce, Don Evans
Secretary of Defense, Donald Rumsfeld
Secretary of Education, Rod Paign
Secretary of Energy, Spencer Abraham
Secretary of Health & Human Services, Tommy Thompson
Secretary of Housing & Urban Development, Mel Martinez
Secretary of Interior, Gale Norton
Department of Justice, John Ashcroft
Secretary of Labor, Elaine Chao
Secretary of State, Colin Powell
Secretary of Transportation, Norman Mineta
Secretary of Treasury, Paul O'Neill
Secretary of Veterans Affairs, Anthony Principi

Cabinet Rank Members
The Vice President, Richard B. Cheney
President's Chief of Staff, Andrew H. Card, Jr.
Environmental Protection Agency, Christie Todd Whitman
Office of Management and Budget Director, Mitchell E. Daniels, Jr.
Office of National Drug Control Policy, John Walters (Nominee)
United States Trade Representative, Ambassador Robert B. Zoellick
Office of Homeland Security, Tom Ridge

Biography of President George W. Bush

George W. Bush is the 43rd President of the United States. Formerly the 46th Governor of the State of Texas, President Bush has earned a reputation as a compassionate conservative who shapes policy based on the principles of limited government, personal responsibility, strong families and local control.

President Bush was born July 6, 1946, and grew up in Midland and Houston, Texas. He received a bachelor's degree from Yale University and a Master of Business Administration from Harvard Business School. He served as an F-102 pilot for the Texas Air National Guard before beginning his career in the oil and gas business in Midland in 1975, working in the energy industry until 1986. After working on his father's successful 1988 presidential campaign, he assembled the group of partners that purchased the Texas Rangers baseball franchise in 1989.

He served as managing general partner of the Texas Rangers until he was elected Governor on November 8, 1994, with 53.5 percent of the vote. In an historic re-election victory, he became the first Texas Governor to be elected to consecutive four-year terms on November 3, 1998, winning 68.6 percent of the vote.

President Bush is pursuing the same common-sense approach and bipartisan spirit that he used in Texas. He has proposed bold initiatives to ensure that America's prosperity has a purpose. He has also addressed improving our nation's public schools by strengthening local control and insisting on accountability; reducing taxes on all taxpayers, especially for those Americans on the fringes of poverty; strengthening the military with better pay, better planning, and better equipment; saving and strengthening Social Security and Medicare by providing seniors with more options; and ushering in the responsibility era in America.

President Bush is married to Laura Welch Bush, a former teacher and librarian, and they have 19-year-old twin daughters, Barbara and Jenna. The Bush family also includes their dogs, Spot and Barney, and a cat, India.

Statement by NATO Secretary General, Lord Robertson

October 8, 2001

Yesterday evening, the United States of America and the United Kingdom began military operations as part of the global campaign against terrorism.

As Secretary General of NATO, I received advance warning. Vice President Dick Cheney telephoned me before the first attacks.

I have just come from a meeting of the North Atlantic Council which met to review the situation and to reaffirm its full support for these targeted actions. The Permanent Representatives of the United States of America and the United Kingdom briefed the Council.

This operation is not directed against the people of Afghanistan. It is designed to strike against al-Qaida terrorist training camps and military installations of the Taliban regime in Afghanistan.

NATO Ambassadors this morning expressed their full support for the actions of the United States and the United Kingdom, which follow the appalling attacks perpetrated against the United States on 11 September 2001. They reiterated their readiness to provide assistance as required. Specifically, they remain fully committed to implement the eight measures agreed on 4 October at the request of the United States.

In this context and following a specific request from the United States, the Allies today agreed that five NATO AWACS aircraft, together with their crews, will deploy to the United States to assist with counter-terrorism operations. This deployment, which was agreed by acclamation this morning, will allow US aircraft currently engaged in these operations in the United States to be released for operations against terrorism elsewhere.

NATO Ambassadors welcomed France's intention to provide increased support by French AWACS aircraft in Bosnia-Herzegovina as backfill in order to facilitate this NATO deployment.

Yesterday's actions were carried out by two NATO Allies. Other NATO Allies have pledged direct military support as this operation unfolds. The Alliance itself will continue to provide military and other support, to consult on the implications for its security, and to take whatever defensive measures are necessary.

The campaign to eradicate terrorism has reached a new stage. It will be pursued on many fronts with determination and with patience. The Alliance stands ready to play its role. I will be consulting over the next couple of days, first of all with Prime Minister Chrétien in Canada this evening and I will personally congratulate and commend the offers of support that have been made by Canada at this time and indeed the support that has already been given by this country. And on Wednesday I will be in the White House to meet President Bush. I will be there first and foremost to express sympathy to his nation on the eve of the month's anniversary of these tragic attrocities but also to pledge the whole-hearted support of the entire NATO Alliance for America at this time of need.

Article 5 of the Washington Treaty

The Parties agree that an armed attack against one or more of them in Europe or North America shall be considered an attack against them all and consequently they agree that, if such an armed attack occurs, each of them, in exercise of the right of individual or collective self-defence recognised by Article 51 of the Charter of the United Nations, will assist the Party or Parties so attacked by taking forthwith, individually and in concert with the other Parties, such action as it deems necessary, including the use of armed force, to restore and maintain the security of the North Atlantic area.

Any such armed attack and all measures taken as a result thereof shall immediately be reported to the Security Council. Such measures shall be terminated when the Security Council has taken the measures necessary to restore and maintain international peace and security.

NATO's Strategic Concept recognises the risks to the Alliance posed by terrorism.

What does Article 5 mean?

Article 5 is at the basis of a fundamental principle of the North Atlantic Treaty Organisation. It provides that if a NATO Ally is the victim of an armed attack, each and every other member of the Alliance will consider this act of violence as an armed attack against all members and will take the actions it deems necessary to assist the Ally attacked.

This is the principle of collective defence.

Article 5 and the case of the terrorist attacks against the United States: The United States has been the object of brutal terrorist attacks. It immediately consulted with the other members of the Alliance. The Alliance determined that the US had been the object of an armed attack. The Alliance therefore agreed that if it was determined that this attack was directed from abroad, it would be regarded as covered by Article 5. NATO Secretary General, Lord Robertson, subsequently informed the Secretary-General of the United Nations of the Alliance's decision.

Article 5 has thus been invoked, but no determination has yet been made whether the attack against the United States was directed from abroad. If such a determination is made, each Ally will then consider what assistance it should provide. In practice, there will be consultations among the Allies. Any collective action by NATO will be decided by the North Atlantic Council. The United States can also carry out independent actions, consistent with its rights and obligations under the UN Charter.

Allies can provide any form of assistance they deem necessary to respond to the situation. This assistance is not necessarily military and depends on the material resources of each country. Each individual member determines how it will contribute and will consult with the other members, bearing in mind that the ultimate aim is to "to restore and maintain the security of the North Atlantic area".

By invoking Article 5, NATO members have shown their solidarity toward the United States and condemned, in the strongest possible way, the terrorist attacks against the United States on 11 September.

If the conditions are met for the application of Article 5, NATO Allies will decide how to assist the United States. (Many Allies have clearly offered emergency assistance). Each Ally is obliged to assist the United States by taking forward, individually and in concert with other Allies, such action as it deems necessary. This is an individual obligation on each Ally and each Ally is responsible for determining what it deems necessary in these particular circumstances.

No collective action will be taken by NATO until further consultations are held and further decisions are made by the the North Atlantic Council.

Statement by the NATO-Ukraine Commission

The NATO-Ukraine Commission extends its deepest condolences to the families and victims of the barbaric acts of terrorism committed against the United States of America on 11 September 2001. These attacks, unprecedented in scale and horror, were directed against the very foundation of democracy and freedom throughout the world.

NATO and Ukraine condemn in the strongest possible terms these atrocities, and stand united in their commitment to ensure that those responsible are brought to justice and punished. In the spirit of its distinctive partnership with NATO, Ukraine stands ready to contribute fully to this effort.

NATO and Ukraine appeal to the entire international community to undertake all measures to combat the scourge of terrorism.

House of Commons Statement by Tony Blair, the Prime Minister on Events in the USA

September 14, 2001

Mr. Speaker, I am grateful that you agreed to the recall of Parliament to debate the hideous and foul events in New York, Washington and Pennsylvania that took place on Tuesday 11 September.

I thought it particularly important in view of the fact that these attacks were not just attacks upon people and buildings; nor even merely upon the USA; these were attacks on the basic democratic values in which we all believe so passionately and on the civilised world. It is therefore right that Parliament, the fount of our own democracy, makes its democratic voice heard.

There will be different shades of opinion heard today. That again is as it should be.

But let us unite in agreeing this: what happened in the United States on Tuesday was an act of wickedness for which there can never be justification. Whatever the cause, whatever the perversion of religious feeling, whatever the political belief, to inflict such terror on the world; to take the lives of so many innocent and defenceless men, women, and children, can never ever be justified.

Let us unite too, with the vast majority of decent people throughout the world, in sending our condolences to the government and the people of America. They are our friends and allies. We the British are a people that stand by our friends in time of need, trial and tragedy, and we do so without hesitation now.

The events are now sickeningly familiar to us. Starting at 08:45 US time, two hijacked planes were flown straight into the twin towers of the

World Trade Centre in New York. Shortly afterwards at 09:43, another hijacked plane was flown into the Pentagon in Washington.

At 10:05 the first tower collapsed; at 10:28 the second; later another building at the World Trade Center. The heart of New York's financial district was devastated, carnage, death and injury everywhere.

Around 10:30 we heard reports that a fourth hijacked aircraft had crashed south of Pittsburgh.

I would like on behalf of the British people to express our admiration for the selfless bravery of the New York and American emergency services, many of whom lost their lives. As we speak, the total death toll is still unclear, but it amounts to several thousands.

Because the World Trade Center was the home of many big financial firms, and because many of their employees are British, whoever committed these acts of terrorism will have murdered at least a hundred British citizens, maybe many more. Murder of British people in New York is no different in nature from their murder in the heart of Britain itself. In the most direct sense, therefore, we have not just an interest but an obligation to bring those responsible to account.

To underline the scale of the loss we are talking about we can think back to some of the appalling tragedies this House has spoken of in the recent past. We can recall the grief aroused by the tragedy at Lockerbie, in which 270 people were killed, 44 of them British. In Omagh, the last terrorist incident to lead to a recall of Parliament, 29 people lost their lives. Each life lost a tragedy. Each one of these events a nightmare for our country. But the death toll we are confronting here is of a different order.

In the Falklands War 255 British Service men perished. During the Gulf War we lost 47.

In this case, we are talking here about a tragedy of epoch making proportions.

And as the scale of this calamity becomes clearer, I fear that there will be many a community in our country where heart-broken families are grieving the loss of a loved one. I have asked the Secretary of State to ensure that everything they need by way of practical support for them is being done.

Here in Britain, we have instituted certain precautionary measures of security. We have tightened security measures at all British airports, and ensured that no plane can take off unless their security is assured. We have temporarily redirected air traffic so that planes do not fly over central London. City Airport is reopening this morning.

We have also been conscious of the possibility of economic disruption. Some sectors like the airlines and insurance industry will be badly affected. But financial markets have quickly stabilised. The oil producers have helped keep the oil price steady. Business is proceeding as far as possible, as normal.

There are three things we must now take forward urgently.

First, we must bring to justice those responsible. Rightly, President Bush and the US Government have proceeded with care. They did not lash out. They did not strike first and think afterwards. Their very deliberation is a measure of the seriousness of their intent.

They, together with allies, will want to identify, with care, those responsible. This is a judgement that must and will be based on hard evidence.

Once that judgement is made, the appropriate action can be taken. It will be determined, it will take time, it will continue over time until this menace is properly dealt with and its machinery of terror destroyed.

But one thing should be very clear. By their acts, these terrorists and those behind them have made themselves the enemies of the civilised world.

The objective will be to bring to account those who have organised, aided, abetted and incited this act of infamy; and those that harbour or help them have a choice: either to cease their protection of our enemies; or be treated as an enemy themselves.

Secondly, this is a moment when every difference between nations, every divergence of interest, every irritant in our relations, are put to one side in one common endeavour. The world should stand together against this outrage.

NATO has already, for the first time since it was founded in 1949, invoked Article 5 and determined that this attack in America will be considered as an attack against the Alliance as a whole.

The UN Security Council on Wednesday passed a resolution which set out its readiness to take all necessary steps to combat terrorism.

From Russia, China, the EU, from Arab states, from Asia and the Americas, from every continent of the world has come united condemnation. This solidarity should be maintained and translated into support for action.

We do not yet know the exact origin of this evil. But, if, as appears likely, it is so-called Islamic fundamentalists, we know they do not speak or act for the vast majority of decent law-abiding Muslims throughout the world. I say to our Arab and Muslim friends: neither you nor Islam is responsible for this; on the contrary, we know you share our shock at this terrorism; and we ask you as friends to make common cause with us in defeating this barbarism that is totally foreign to the true spirit and teachings of Islam.

And I would add that, now more than ever, we have reason not to let the Middle East Peace Process slip still further but if at all possible to reinvigorate it and move it forward.

Thirdly, whatever the nature of the immediate response to these terrible events in America, we need to re-think dramatically the scale and nature of the action the world takes to combat terrorism.

We know a good deal about many of these terror groups. But as a world we have not been effective at dealing with them.

And of course it is difficult. We are democratic. They are not. We have respect for human life. They do not. We hold essentially liberal values. They do not. As we look into these issues it is important that we never lose sight of our basic values. But we have to understand the nature of the enemy and act accordingly.

Civil liberties are a vital part of our country, and of our world. But the most basic liberty of all is the right of the ordinary citizen to go about their business free from fear or terror. That liberty has been denied, in the cruellest way imaginable, to the passengers aboard the hijacked planes, to those who perished in the trade towers and the Pentagon, to the hundreds of rescue workers killed as they tried to help.

So we need to look once more nationally and internationally at extradition laws, and the mechanisms for international justice; at how these terrorist groups are financed and their money laundered, and the links between terror and crime and we need to frame a response that will work, and hold internationally.

For this form of terror knows no mercy; no pity, and it knows no boundaries.

And let us make this reflection. A week ago, anyone suggesting terrorists would kill thousands of innocent people in downtown New York would have been dismissed as alarmist. It happened. We know that these groups are fanatics, capable of killing without discrimination. The limits on the numbers they kill and their methods of killing are not governed by morality. The limits are only practical or technical. We know, that they would, if they could, go further and use chemical or biological or even nuclear weapons of mass destruction. We know, also, that there are groups or people, occasionally states, who trade the technology and capability for such weapons.

It is time this trade was exposed, disrupted, and stamped out. We have been warned by the events of 11 September. We should act on the warning.

So there is a great deal to do and many details to be filled in, much careful work to be undertaken over the coming days, weeks and months.

We need to mourn the dead; and then act to protect the living.

Terrorism has taken on a new and frightening aspect.

The people perpetrating it wear the ultimate badge of the fanatic: they are prepared to commit suicide in pursuit of their beliefs.

Our beliefs are the very opposite of the fanatics. We believe in reason, democracy and tolerance.

These beliefs are the foundation of our civilised world. They are enduring, they have served us well and as history has shown we have been prepared to fight, when necessary to defend them. But the fanatics should know: we hold these beliefs every bit as strongly as they hold theirs.

Now is the time to show it.

Speech by Tony Blair, Prime Minister, Labour Party Conference, Brighton

October 2, 2001

In retrospect the Millennium marked only a moment in time. It was the events of 11 September that marked a turning point in history, where we confront the dangers of the future and assess the choices facing humankind. It was a tragedy. An act of evil. From this nation, goes our deepest sympathy and prayers for the victims and our profound solidarity with the American people.

We were with you at the first. We will stay with you to the last.

Just two weeks ago, in New York, after the church service I met some of the families of the British victims.

It was in many ways a very British occasion. Tea and biscuits. It was raining outside. Around the edge of the room, strangers making small talk, trying to be normal people in an abnormal situation. And as you crossed the room, you felt the longing and sadness; hands clutching photos of sons and daughters, wives and husbands; imploring you to believe them when they said there was still an outside chance of their loved ones being found alive, when you knew in truth that all hope was gone.

And then a middle aged mother looks you in the eyes and tells you her only son has died, and asks you why?

I tell you: you do not feel like the most powerful person in the country at times like that.

Because there is no answer. There is no justification for their pain. Their son did nothing wrong. The woman, seven months pregnant, whose child will never know its father, did nothing wrong.

They don't want revenge. They want something better in memory of their loved ones.

I believe their memorial can and should be greater than simply the punishment of the guilty. It is that out of the shadow of this evil, should emerge lasting good: destruction of the machinery of terrorism wherever it is found; hope amongst all nations of a new beginning where we seek to resolve differences in a calm and ordered way; greater understanding between nations and between faiths; and above all justice and prosperity for the poor and dispossessed, so that people everywhere can see the chance of a better future through the hard work and creative power of the free citizen, not the violence and savagery of the fanatic.

I know that here in Britain people are anxious, even a little frightened. I understand that. People know we must act but they worry what might follow.

They worry about the economy and talk of recession.

And, of course there are dangers; it is a new situation.

But the fundamentals of the US, British and European economies are strong.

Every reasonable measure of internal security is being undertaken.

Our way of life is a great deal stronger and will last a great deal longer than the actions of fanatics, small in number and now facing a unified world against them.

People should have confidence.

This is a battle with only one outcome: our victory not theirs.

What happened on 11 September was without parallel in the bloody history of terrorism.

Within a few hours, up to 7000 people were annihilated, the commercial centre of New York was reduced to rubble and in Washington and Pennsylvania further death and horror on an unimaginable scale. Let no one say this was a blow for Islam when the blood of innocent Muslims was shed along with those of the Christian, Jewish and other faiths around the world.

We know those responsible. In Afghanistan are scores of training camps for the export of terror. Chief amongst the sponsors and organisers is Usama Bin Laden.

He is supported, shielded and given succour by the Taliban regime.

Two days before the 11 September attacks, Masood, the Leader of the

Opposition Northern Alliance, was assassinated by two suicide bombers. Both were linked to Bin Laden. Some may call that coincidence. I call it payment - payment in the currency these people deal in: blood.

Be in no doubt: Bin Laden and his people organised this atrocity. The Taliban aid and abet him. He will not desist from further acts of terror. They will not stop helping him.

Whatever the dangers of the action we take, the dangers of inaction are far, far greater.

Look for a moment at the Taliban regime. It is undemocratic. That goes without saying.

There is no sport allowed, or television or photography. No art or culture is permitted. All other faiths, all other interpretations of Islam are ruthlessly suppressed. Those who practice their faith are imprisoned. Women are treated in a way almost too revolting to be credible. First driven out of university; girls not allowed to go to school; no legal rights; unable to go out of doors without a man. Those that disobey are stoned.

There is now no contact permitted with western agencies, even those delivering food. The people live in abject poverty. It is a regime founded on fear and funded on the drugs trade. The biggest drugs hoard in the world is in Afghanistan, controlled by the Taliban. Ninety per cent of the heroin on British streets originates in Afghanistan.

The arms the Taliban are buying today are paid for with the lives of young British people buying their drugs on British streets.

That is another part of their regime that we should seek to destroy.

So what do we do?

Don't overreact some say. We aren't.

We haven't lashed out. No missiles on the first night just for effect.

Don't kill innocent people. We are not the ones who waged war on the innocent. We seek the guilty.

Look for a diplomatic solution. There is no diplomacy with Bin Laden or the Taliban regime.

State an ultimatum and get their response. We stated the ultimatum; they haven't responded.

Understand the causes of terror. Yes, we should try, but let there be no moral ambiguity about this: nothing could ever justify the events of 11 September, and it is to turn justice on its head to pretend it could.

The action we take will be proportionate; targeted; we will do all we humanly can to avoid civilian casualties. But understand what we are dealing with. Listen to the calls of those passengers on the planes. Think of the children on them, told they were going to die.

Think of the cruelty beyond our comprehension as amongst the screams and the anguish of the innocent, those hijackers drove at full throttle planes laden with fuel into buildings where tens of thousands worked.

They have no moral inhibition on the slaughter of the innocent. If they could have murdered not 7,000 but 70,000 does anyone doubt they would have done so and rejoiced in it?

There is no compromise possible with such people, no meeting of minds, no point of understanding with such terror.

Just a choice: defeat it or be defeated by it. And defeat it we must.

Any action taken will be against the terrorist network of Bin Laden.

As for the Taliban, they can surrender the terrorists; or face the consequences and again in any action the aim will be to eliminate their military hardware, cut off their finances, disrupt their supplies, target their troops, not civilians. We will put a trap around the regime.

I say to the Taliban: surrender the terrorists, or surrender power. It's your choice.

We will take action at every level, national and international, in the UN, in G8, in the EU, in NATO, in every regional grouping in the world, to strike at international terrorism wherever it exists.

For the first time, the UN Security Council has imposed mandatory obligations on all UN members to cut off terrorist financing and end safe havens for terrorists.

Those that finance terror, those who launder their money, those that cover their tracks are every bit as guilty as the fanatic who commits the final act.

Here in this country and in other nations round the world, laws will be changed, not to deny basic liberties but to prevent their abuse and protect the most basic liberty of all: freedom from terror. New extradition laws will be introduced; new rules to ensure asylum is not a front for terrorist entry. This country is proud of its tradition in giving asylum to those fleeing tyranny. We will always do so. But we have a duty to protect the system from abuse.

It must be overhauled radically so that from now on, those who abide by the rules get help and those that don't, can no longer play the system to gain unfair advantage over others.

Round the world, 11 September is bringing Governments and people to reflect, consider and change. And in this process, amidst all the talk of war and action, there is another dimension appearing.

There is a coming together. The power of community is asserting itself. We are realising how fragile are our frontiers in the face of the world's new challenges.

Today conflicts rarely stay within national boundaries.

Today a tremor in one financial market is repeated in the markets of the world.

Today confidence is global; either its presence or its absence.

Today the threat is chaos; because for people with work to do, family life to balance, mortgages to pay, careers to further, pensions to provide, the yearning is for order and stability and if it doesn't exist elsewhere, it is unlikely to exist here.

I have long believed this interdependence defines the new world we live in.

People say: we are only acting because it's the USA that was attacked. Double standards, they say. But when Milosevic embarked on the ethnic cleansing of Muslims in Kosovo, we acted.

The sceptics said it was pointless, we'd make matters worse, we'd make Milosovic stronger and look what happened, we won, the refugees went home, the policies of ethnic cleansing were reversed and one of the great dictators of the last century, will see justice in this century.

And I tell you if Rwanda happened again today as it did in 1993, when a million people were slaughtered in cold blood, we would have a moral duty to act there also. We were there in Sierra Leone when a murderous group of gangsters threatened its democratically elected Government and people.

And we as a country should, and I as Prime Minister do, give thanks for the brilliance, dedication and sheer professionalism of the British Armed Forces.

We can't do it all. Neither can the Americans.

But the power of the international community could, together, if it chose to.

It could, with our help, sort out the blight that is the continuing conflict in the Democratic Republic of the Congo, where three million people have died through war or famine in the last decade.

A Partnership for Africa, between the developed and developing world based around the New African Initiative, is there to be done if we find the will.

On our side: provide more aid, untied to trade; write off debt; help with good governance and infrastructure; training to the soldiers, with UN blessing, in conflict resolution; encouraging investment; and access to our markets so that we practise the free trade we are so fond of preaching.

But it's a deal: on the African side: true democracy, no more excuses for dictatorship, abuses of human rights; no tolerance of bad governance, from the endemic corruption of some states, to the activities of Mr Mugabe's henchmen in Zimbabwe. Proper commercial, legal and financial systems.

The will, with our help, to broker agreements for peace and provide troops to police them.

The state of Africa is a scar on the conscience of the world. But if the world as a community focused on it, we could heal it. And if we don't, it will become deeper and angrier.

We could defeat climate change if we chose to. Kyoto is right. We will implement it and call upon all other nations to do so.

But it's only a start. With imagination, we could use or find the technologies that create energy without destroying our planet; we could provide work and trade without deforestation.

If humankind was able, finally, to make industrial progress without the factory conditions of the 19th Century; surely we have the wit and will to develop economically without despoiling the very environment we depend upon. And if we wanted to, we could breathe new life into the Middle East Peace Process and we must.

The state of Israel must be given recognition by all; freed from terror; know that it is accepted as part of the future of the Middle East not its very existence under threat. The Palestinians must have justice, the chance to prosper and in their own land, as equal partners with Israel in that future.

We know that. It is the only way, just as we know in our own peace process, in Northern Ireland, there will be no unification of Ireland except by consent - and there will be no return to the days of unionist or Protestant supremacy because those days have no place in the modern world. So the unionists must accept justice and equality for nationalists.

The Republicans must show they have given up violence - not just a ceasefire but weapons put beyond use. And not only the Republicans, but those people who call themselves Loyalists, but who by acts of terrorism, sully the name of the United Kingdom.

We know this also. The values we believe in should shine through what we do in Afghanistan.

To the Afghan people we make this commitment. The conflict will not be the end. We will not walk away, as the outside world has done so many times before.

If the Taliban regime changes, we will work with you to make sure its successor is one that is broad-based, that unites all ethnic groups, and that offers some way out of the miserable poverty that is your present existence.

And, more than ever now, with every bit as much thought and planning, we will assemble a humanitarian coalition alongside the military coalition so that inside and outside Afghanistan, the refugees, four and one-half million on the move even before 11 September, are given shelter, food and help during the winter months.

The world community must show as much its capacity for compassion as for force.

The critics will say: but how can the world be a community?
Nations act in their own self-interest. Of course they do. But what is the lesson of the financial markets, climate change, international terrorism, nuclear proliferation or world trade? It is that our self-interest and our mutual interests are today inextricably woven together.

This is the politics of globalisation.

I realise why people protest against globalisation.

We watch aspects of it with trepidation. We feel powerless, as if we were now pushed to and fro by forces far beyond our control.

But there's a risk that political leaders, faced with street demonstrations, pander to the argument rather than answer it. The demonstrators are right to say there's injustice, poverty, environmental degradation.

But globalisation is a fact and, by and large, it is driven by people.

Not just in finance, but in communication, in technology, increasingly in culture, in recreation. In the world of the internet, information technology and TV, there will be globalisation. And in trade, the problem is not there's too much of it; on the contrary there's too little of it.

The issue is not how to stop globalisation.

The issue is how we use the power of community to combine it with justice. If globalisation works only for the benefit of the few, then it will fail and will deserve to fail. But if we follow the principles that have served us so well at home - that power, wealth and opportunity must be in the hands of the many, not the few - if we make that our guiding light for the global economy, then it will be a force for good and an international movement that we should take pride in leading.

Because the alternative to globalisation is isolation.

Confronted by this reality, round the world, nations are instinctively drawing together. In Quebec, all the countries of North and South America deciding to make one huge free trade area, rivalling Europe. In Asia, ASEAN. In Europe, the most integrated grouping of all, we are now 15 nations. Another 12 countries negotiating to join, and more beyond that.

A new relationship between Russia and Europe is beginning.

And will not India and China, each with three times as many citizens as the whole of the EU put together, once their economies have developed sufficiently as they will do, not reconfigure entirely the geopolitics of the world and in our lifetime?

That is why, with 60 per cent of our trade dependent on Europe, three million jobs tied up with Europe, much of our political weight engaged in Europe, it would be a fundamental denial of our true national interest to turn our backs on Europe.

We will never let that happen.

For 50 years, Britain has, uncharacteristically, followed not led in Europe.

At each and every step. There are debates central to our future coming up: how we reform European economic policy; how we take forward European defence; how we fight organised crime and terrorism.

Britain needs its voice strong in Europe and bluntly Europe needs a strong Britain, rock solid in our alliance with the USA, yet determined to play its full part in shaping Europe's destiny.

We should only be part of the single currency if the economic conditions are met. They are not window-dressing for a political decision. They are fundamental. But if they are met, we should join, and if met in this Parliament, we should have the courage of our argument, to ask the British people for their consent in this Parliament.

Europe is not a threat to Britain. Europe is an opportunity.

It is in taking the best of the Anglo-Saxon and European models of development that Britain's hope of a prosperous future lies. The American spirit of enterprise; the European spirit of solidarity. We have, here also, an opportunity. Not just to build bridges politically, but economically.

What is the answer to the current crisis? Not isolationism but the world coming together with America as a community.

What is the answer to Britain's relations with Europe? Not opting out, but being leading members of a community in which, in alliance with others, we gain strength.

What is the answer to Britain's future? Not each person for themselves, but working together as a community to ensure that everyone, not just the privileged few get the chance to succeed.

This is an extraordinary moment for progressive politics.

Our values are the right ones for this age: the power of community, solidarity, the collective ability to further the individual's interests.

People ask me if I think ideology is dead. My answer is: In the sense of rigid forms of economic and social theory, yes.

The 20th Century killed those ideologies and their passing causes little regret. But, in the sense of a governing idea in politics, based on values, no. The governing idea of modern social democracy is community. Founded on the principles of social justice. That people should rise according to merit not birth; that the test of any decent society is not the contentment of the wealthy and strong, but the commitment to the poor and weak.

But values aren't enough. The mantle of leadership comes at a price: the courage to learn and change; to show how values that stand for all ages, can be applied in a way relevant to each age.

Our politics only succeed when the realism is as clear as the idealism.

This Party's strength today comes from the journey of change and learning we have made.

We learnt that however much we strive for peace, we need strong defence capability where a peaceful approach fails.

We learnt that equality is about equal worth, not equal outcomes.

Today our idea of society is shaped around mutual responsibility; a deal, an agreement between citizens not a one-way gift, from the well-off to the dependent.

Our economic and social policy today owes as much to the liberal social democratic tradition of Lloyd George, Keynes and Beveridge as to the socialist principles of the 1945 Government.

Just over a decade ago, people asked if Labour could ever win again. Today they ask the same question of the Opposition. Painful though that journey of change has been, it has been worth it, every stage of the way.

On this journey, the values have never changed. The aims haven't. Our aims would be instantly recognisable to every Labour leader from Keir Hardie onwards. But the means do change.

The journey hasn't ended. It never ends. The next stage for New Labour is not backwards; it is renewing ourselves again. Just after the election, an old colleague of mine said: "Come on Tony, now we've won again, can't we drop all this New Labour and do what we believe in?"

I said: "It's worse than you think. I really do believe in it".

We didn't revolutionise British economic policy - Bank of England independence, tough spending rules - for some managerial reason or as a clever wheeze to steal Tory clothes.

We did it because the victims of economic incompetence - 15% interest rates, 3 million unemployed- are hard-working families. They are the ones - and even more so, now - with tough times ahead - that the economy should be run for, not speculators, or currency dealers or senior executives whose pay packets don't seem to bear any resemblance to the performance of their companies.

Economic competence is the pre-condition of social justice.

We have legislated for fairness at work, like the minimum wage which people struggled a century for. But we won't give up the essential flexibility of our economy or our commitment to enterprise.

Why? Because in a world leaving behind mass production, where technology revolutionises not just companies but whole industries, almost overnight, enterprise creates the jobs people depend on.

We have boosted pensions, child benefit, family incomes. We will do more. But our number one priority for spending is and will remain education.

Why? Because in the new markets countries like Britain can only create wealth by brain power not low wages and sweatshop labour.

We have cut youth unemployment by 75 percent.

By more than any Government before us. But we refuse to pay benefit to those who refuse to work. Why? Because the welfare that works is welfare that helps people to help themselves.

The graffiti, the vandalism, the burnt out cars, the street corner drug dealers, the teenage mugger just graduating from the minor school of crime: we're not old fashioned or right-wing to take action against this social menace.

We're standing up for the people we represent, who play by the rules and have a right to expect others to do the same.

And especially at this time let us say: we celebrate the diversity in our country, get strength from the cultures and races that go to make up Britain today; and racist abuse and racist attacks have no place in the Britain we believe in.

All these policies are linked by a common thread of principle.

Now with this second term, our duty is not to sit back and bask in it. It is across the board, in competition policy, enterprise, pensions, criminal justice, the civil service and of course public services, to go still further in the journey of change. All for the same reason: to allow us to deliver social justice in the modern world.

Public services are the power of community in action.

They are social justice made real. The child with a good education flourishes. The child given a poor education lives with it for the rest of their life. How much talent and ability and potential do we waste? How many children never know not just the earning power of a good education but the joy of art and culture and the stretching of imagination and horizons which true education brings? Poor education is a personal tragedy and national scandal.

Yet even now, with all the progress of recent years, a quarter of 11 year olds fail their basic tests and almost a half of 16 year olds don't get five decent GCSEs.

The NHS meant that for succeeding generations, anxiety was lifted from their shoulders. For millions who get superb treatment still, the NHS remains the ultimate symbol of social justice.

But for every patient waiting in pain, that can't get treatment for cancer or a heart condition or in desperation ends up paying for their operation, that patient's suffering is the ultimate social injustice.

And the demands on the system are ever greater. Children need to be better and better educated.

People live longer. There is a vast array of new treatment available.

And expectations are higher. This is a consumer age. People don't take what they're given. They demand more.

We're not alone in this. All round the world governments are struggling with the same problems.

So what is the solution? Yes, public services need more money. We are putting in the largest ever increases in NHS, education and transport spending in the next few years; and on the police too. We will keep to those spending plans. And I say in all honesty to the country: if we want that to continue and the choice is between investment and tax cuts, then investment must come first. There is a simple truth we all know. For decades there has been chronic under-investment in British public services. Our historic mission is to put that right; and the historic shift represented by the election of June 7 was that investment to provide quality public services for all comprehensively defeated short-term tax cuts for the few.

We need better pay and conditions for the staff; better incentives for recruitment; and for retention. We're getting them and recruitment is rising.

This year, for the first time in nearly a decade, public sector pay will rise faster than private sector pay.

And we are the only major government in Europe this year to be increasing public spending on health and education as a percentage of our national income.

This Party believes in public services; believes in the ethos of public service; and believes in the dedication the vast majority of public servants show; and the proof of it is that we're spending more, hiring more and paying more than ever before.

Public servants don't do it for money or glory. They do it because they find fulfilment in a child well taught or a patient well cared-for; or a community made safer and we salute them for it.

All that is true. But this is also true.

That often they work in systems and structures that are hopelessly old fashioned or even worse, work against the very goals they aim for.

There are schools, with exactly the same social intake. One does well; the other badly.

There are hospitals with exactly the same patient mix. One performs well; the other badly.

Without reform, more money and pay won't succeed.

First, we need a national framework of accountability, inspection; and minimum standards of delivery.

Second, within that framework, we need to free up local leaders to be able to innovate, develop and be creative.

Third, there should be far greater flexibility in the terms and conditions of employment of public servants.

Fourth, there has to be choice for the user of public services and the ability, where provision of the service fails, to have an alternative provider.

If schools want to develop or specialise in a particular area; or hire classroom assistants or computer professionals as well as teachers, let them. If in a Primary Care Trust, doctors can provide minor surgery or physiotherapists see patients otherwise referred to a consultant, let them.

There are too many old demarcations, especially between nurses, doctors and consultants; too little use of the potential of new technology; too much bureaucracy, too many outdated practices, too great an adherence to the way we've always done it rather than the way public servants would like to do it if they got the time to think and the freedom to act.

It's not reform that is the enemy of public services. It's the status quo.

Part of that reform programme is partnership with the private or voluntary sector.

Let's get one thing clear. Nobody is talking about privatising the NHS or schools.

Nobody believes the private sector is a panacea.

There are great examples of public service and poor examples. There are excellent private sector companies and poor ones. There are areas where the private sector has worked well; and areas where, as with parts of the railways, it's been a disaster.

Where the private sector is used, it should not make a profit simply by cutting the wages and conditions of its staff.

But where the private sector can help lever in vital capital investment, where it helps raise standards, where it improves the public service as a public service, then to set up some dogmatic barrier to using it, is to let down the very people who most need our public services to improve.

This programme of reform is huge: in the NHS, education, including student finance, - we have to find a better way to combine state funding and student contributions - ; criminal justice; and transport.

I regard it as being as important for the country as Clause IV's reform was for the Party, and obviously far more important for the lives of the people we serve.

And it is a vital test for the modern Labour Party

If people lose faith in public services, be under no illusion as to what will happen.

There is a different approach waiting in the wings. Cut public spending drastically; let those that can afford to, buy their own services; and those that can't, will depend on a demoralised, sink public service. That would be a denial of social justice on a massive scale.

It would be contrary to the very basis of community.

So this is a battle of values. Let's have that battle but not amongst ourselves. The real fight is between those who believe in strong public services and those who don't.

That's the fight worth having.

In all of this, at home and abroad, the same beliefs throughout: that we are a community of people, whose self-interest and mutual interest at crucial points merge, and that it is through a sense of justice that community is born and nurtured.

And what does this concept of justice consist of?

Fairness, people all of equal worth, of course. But also reason and tolerance. Justice has no favourites; not amongst nations, peoples or faiths.

When we act to bring to account those that committed the atrocity of

11 September, we do so, not out of bloodlust.

We do so because it is just. We do not act against Islam. The true followers of Islam are our brothers and sisters in this struggle. Bin Laden is no more obedient to the proper teaching of the Koran than those Crusaders of the 12th Century who pillaged and murdered, represented the teaching of the Gospel.

It is time the West confronted its ignorance of Islam. Jews, Muslims and Christians are all children of Abraham.

This is the moment to bring the faiths closer together in understanding of our common values and heritage, a source of unity and strength.

It is time also for parts of Islam to confront prejudice against America and not only Islam but parts of western societies too.
America has its faults as a society, as we have ours.

But I think of the Union of America born out of the defeat of slavery.

I think of its Constitution, with its inalienable rights granted to every citizen still a model for the world.

I think of a black man, born in poverty, who became Chief of their Armed Forces and is now Secretary of State Colin Powell and I wonder frankly whether such a thing could have happened here.

I think of the Statue of Liberty and how many refugees, migrants and the impoverished passed its light and felt that if not for them, for their children, a new world could indeed be theirs.

I think of a country where people who do well, don't have questions asked about their accent, their class, their beginnings but have admiration for what they have done and the success they've achieved.

I think of those New Yorkers I met, still in shock, but resolute; the fire fighters and police, mourning their comrades but still head held high.

I think of all this and I reflect: yes, America has its faults, but it is a free country, a democracy, it is our ally and some of the reaction to 11 September betrays a hatred of America that shames those that feel it.

So I believe this is a fight for freedom. And I want to make it a fight for justice too.

Justice not only to punish the guilty. But justice to bring those same values of democracy and freedom to people round the world.

And I mean: freedom, not only in the narrow sense of personal liberty but in the broader sense of each individual having the economic and social freedom to develop their potential to the full. That is what community means, founded on the equal worth of all.

The starving, the wretched, the dispossessed, the ignorant, those living in want and squalor from the deserts of Northern Africa to the slums of Gaza, to the mountain ranges of Afghanistan: they too are our cause.

This is a moment to seize.

The Kaleidoscope has been shaken. The pieces are in flux. Soon they will settle again.

Before they do, let us re-order this world around us.

Today, humankind has the science and technology to destroy itself or to provide prosperity to all.

Yet science can't make that choice for us.

Only the moral power of a world acting as a community, can.

"By the strength of our common endeavour we achieve more together than we can alone".

For those people who lost their lives on 11 September and those that mourn them; now is the time for the strength to build that community. Let that be their memorial.

Responsibility for the Terrorist Atrocities in the United States, September 11, 2001
Presented by Tony Blair

This document does not purport to provide a prosecutable case against Usama Bin Laden in a court of law. Intelligence often cannot be used evidentially, due both to the strict rules of admissibility and to the need to protect the safety of sources. But on the basis of all the information available HMG is confident of its conclusions as expressed in this document.

RESPONSIBILITY FOR THE TERRORIST ATROCITIES IN THE UNITED STATES, 11 SEPTEMBER 2001

INTRODUCTION

1. The clear conclusions reached by the government are:
   - Usama Bin Laden and Al Qaida, the terrorist network which he heads, planned and carried out the atrocities on 11 September 2001;
   - Usama Bin Laden and Al Qaida retain the will and resources to carry out further atrocities;
   - the United Kingdom, and United Kingdom nationals are potential targets; and
   - Usama Bin Laden and Al Qaida were able to commit these atrocities because of their close alliance with the Taleban régime, which allowed them to operate with impunity in pursuing their terrorist activity.

2. The material in respect of 1998 and the USS Cole comes from indictments and intelligence sources. The material in respect of 11 September comes from intelligence and the criminal investigation to date. The details of some aspects cannot be given, but the facts are clear from the intelligence.

3. The document does not contain the totality of the material known to HMG, given the continuing and absolute need to protect intelligence sources.

SUMMARY

4. The relevant facts show:

Background
   - Al Qaida is a terrorist organisation with ties to a global network, which has been in existence for over 10 years. It was founded, and has been led at all times, by Usama Bin Laden.
   - Usama Bin Laden and Al Qaida have been engaged in a jihad against the United States, and its allies. One of their stated aims is the murder of US citizens,

and attacks on America's allies.

• Usama Bin Laden and Al Qaida have been based in Afghanistan since 1996, but have a network of operations throughout the world. The network includes training camps, warehouses, communication facilities and commercial operations able to raise significant sums of money to support its activity. That activity includes substantial exploitation of the illegal drugs trade from Afghanistan.

• Usama Bin Laden's Al Qaida and the Taleban régime have a close and mutually dependent alliance. Usama Bin Laden and Al Qaida provide the Taleban régime with material, financial and military support. They jointly exploit the drugs trade. The Taleban régime allows Bin Laden to operate his terrorist training camps and activities from Afghanistan, protects him from attacks from outside, and protects the drugs stockpiles. Usama Bin Laden could not operate his terrorist activities without the alliance and support of the Taleban régime. The Taleban's strength would be seriously weakened without Usama Bin Laden's military and financial support.

• Usama Bin Laden and Al Qaida have the capability to execute major terrorist attacks.

• Usama Bin Laden has claimed credit for the attack on US soldiers in Somalia in October 1993, which killed 18; for the attack on the US Embassies in Kenya and Tanzania in August 1998 which killed 224 and injured nearly 5000; and were linked to the attack on the USS Cole on 12 October 2000, in which 17 crew members were killed and 40 others injured.

• They have sought to acquire nuclear and chemical materials for use as terrorist weapons.

IN RELATION TO THE TERRORIST ATTACKS ON 11 SEPTEMBER

5. After 11 September we learned that, not long before, Bin Laden had indicated he was about to launch a major attack on America. The detailed planning for the terrorist attacks of 11 September was carried out by one of UBL's close associates. Of the 19 hijackers involved in 11 September 2001, it has already been established that at least three had links with Al Qaida. The attacks on 11 September 2001 were similar in both their ambition and intended impact to previous attacks undertaken by Usama Bin laden and Al Qaida, and also had features in common. In particular:

• Suicide attackers
• Co-ordinated attacks on the same day
• The aim to cause maximum American casualties
• Total disregard for other casualties, including Muslim
• Meticulous long-term planning
• Absence of warning.

6. Al Qaida retains the capability and the will to make further attacks on the US and its allies, including the United Kingdom.

7. Al Qaida gives no warning of terrorist attack.

THE FACTS

Usama Bin Laden and Al Qaida

8. In 1989 Usama Bin Laden, and others, founded an international terrorist group known as "Al Qaida" (the Base). At all times he has been the leader of Al Qaida.

9. From 1989 until 1991 Usama Bin Laden was based in Afghanistan and Peshawar, Pakistan. In 1991 he moved to Sudan, where he stayed until 1996. In that year he returned to Afghanistan, where he remains.

The Taleban Regime

10. The Taleban emerged from the Afghan refugee camps in Pakistan in the early 1990s. By 1996 they had captured Kabul. They are still engaged in a bloody civil war to control the whole of Afghanistan. They are led by Mullah Omar.

11. In 1996 Usama Bin Laden moved back to Afghanistan. He established a close relationship with Mullah Omar, and threw his support behind the Taleban. Usama Bin Laden and the Taleban régime have a close alliance on which both depend for their continued existence. They also share the same religious values and vision.

12. Usama Bin Laden has provided the Taleban régime with troops, arms, and money to fight the Northern Alliance. He is closely involved with Taleban military training, planning and operations. He has representatives in the Taleban military command structure. He has also given infrastruture assistance and humanitarian aid. Forces under the control of Usama Bin Laden have fought alongside the Taleban in the civil war in Afghanistan.

13. Omar has provided Bin Laden with a safe haven in which to operate, and has allowed him to establish terrorist training camps in Afghanistan. They jointly exploit the Afghan drugs trade. In return for active Al Qaida support, the Taleban allow Al Qaida to operate freely, including planning, training and preparing for terrorist activity. In addition the Taleban provide security for the stockpiles of drugs.

14. Since 1996, when the Taleban captured Kabul, the United States government has consistently raised with them a whole range of issues, including humanitarian aid and terrorism. Well before 11 September 2001 they had provided evidence to the Taleban of the responsibility of Al Qaida for the terrorist attacks in East Africa. This evidence had been provided to senior leaders of the Taleban at their request.

15. The United States government had made it clear to the Taleban regime that Al Qaida had murdered US citizens, and planned to murder more. The US offered to work with the Taleban to expel the terrorists from Afghanistan. These talks, which have been continuing since 1996, have failed to produce any results.

16. In June 2001, in the face of mounting evidence of the Al Qaida threat, the United States warned the Taleban that it had the right to defend itself and that it would hold the régime responsible for attacks against US citizens by terrorists sheltered in Afghanistan.

17. In this, the United States had the support of the United Nations. The Security Council, in Resolution 1267, condemned Usama Bin Laden for sponsoring international terrorism and operating a network of terrorist camps, and demanded that the Taleban surrender Usama Bin Laden without further delay so that he could be brought to justice.

18. Despite the evidence provided by the US of the responsibility of Usama Bin Laden and Al Qaida for the 1998 East Africa bombings, despite the accurately perceived threats of further atrocities, and despite the demands of the United Nations, the Taleban régime responded by saying no evidence existed against Usama Bin Laden, and that neither he nor his network would be expelled.

19. A former Government official in Afghanistan has described the Taleban and Usama Bin Laden as "two sides of the same coin: Usama cannot exist in Afghanistan without the Taleban and the Taleban cannot exist without Usama."

Al Qaida

20. Al Qaida is dedicated to opposing 'un-Islamic' governments in Muslim countries with force and violence.

21. Al Qaida virulently opposes the United States. Usama Bin Laden has urged and incited his followers to kill American citizens, in the most unequivocal terms.

22. On 12 October 1996 he issued a declaration of jihad as follows:

"The people of Islam have suffered from aggression, iniquity and injustice imposed by the Zionist-Crusader alliance and their collaborators . . .It is the duty now on every tribe in the Arabian peninsula to fight jihad and cleanse the land from these Crusader occupiers. Their wealth is booty to those who kill them. My Muslim brothers: your brothers in Palestine and in the land of the two Holy Places [i.e. Saudi Arabia] are calling upon your help and asking you to take part in fighting against the enemy – the Americans and the Israelis. They are asking you to do whatever you can to expel the enemies out of the sancties of Islam."

Later in the same year he said that

"terrorising the American occupiers [of Islamic Holy Places] is a religious and logical obligation."

In February 1998 he issued and signed a 'fatwa' which included a decree to all Muslims:

". . . the killing of Americans and their civilian and military allies is a religious duty for each and every Muslim to be carried out in whichever country they are until Al Aqsa mosque has been liberated from their grasp and until their armies have left Muslim lands."

In the same 'fatwa' he called on Muslim scholars and their leaders and their youths to

"launch an attack on the American soldiers of Satan."

and concluded:

"We – with God's help – call on every Muslim who believes in God and wishes to be rewarded to comply with God's order to kill Americans and plunder their money whenever and wherever they find it. We also call on Muslims . . . to launch the raid on Satan's US troops and the devil's supporters allying with them, and to displace those who are behind them."

When asked, in 1998, about obtaining chemical or nuclear weapons he said

"acquiring such weapons for the defence of Muslims [was] a religious duty."

In an interview aired on Al Jazira (Doha, Qatar) television he stated:

"Our enemy is every American male, whether he is directly fighting us or paying taxes."

In two interviews broadcast on US television in 1997 and 1998 he referred to the terrorists who carried out the earlier attack on the World Trade Center in 1993 as "role models". He went on to exhort his followers "to take the fighting to America."

23.   From the early 1990s Usama Bin Laden has sought to obtain nuclear and chemical materials for use as weapons of terror.

24. Although US targets are Al Qaida's priority, it also explicitly threatens the United States' allies. References to "Zionist-Crusader alliance and their collaborators," and to "Satan's US troops and the devil's supporters allying with them" are references which unquestionably include the United Kingdom.

25.   There is a continuing threat. Based on our experience of the way the network has operated in the past, other cells, like those that carried out the terrorist attacks on 11 September, must be assumed to exist.

26.   Al Qaida functions both on its own and through a network of other terrorist organisations. These include Egyptian Islamic Jihad and other north African Islamic extremist terrorist groups, and a number of other jihadi groups in other countries including the Sudan, Yemen, Somalia, Pakistan and India. Al Qaida also maintains cells and personnel in a number of other countries to facilitate its activities.

27.   Usama Bin Laden heads the Al Qaida network. Below him is a body known as the Shura, which includes representatives of other terrorist groups, such as Egyptian Islamic Jihad leader Ayman Zawahiri and prominent lieutenants of Bin Laden such as Abu Hafs Al-Masri. Egyptian Islamic Jihad has, in effect, merged with Al Qaida.

28.   In addition to the Shura, Al Qaida has several groups dealing with military, media, financial and Islamic issues.

29.   Mohamed Atef is a member of the group that deals with military and terrorist operations. His duties include principal responsibility for training Al Qaida members.

30.   Members of Al Qaida must make a pledge of allegiance to follow the orders of Usama Bin Laden.

31.   A great deal of evidence about Usama Bin Laden and Al Qaida has been made available in the US indictment for earlier crimes.

32.   Since 1989, Usama Bin Laden has conducted substantial financial and business transactions on behalf of Al Qaida and in pursuit of its goals. These include purchasing land for training camps, purchasing warehouses for the storage of items, including explosives, purchasing communications and electronics equipment, and transporting currency and weapons to members of Al Qaida and associated terrorist groups in countries throughout the world.

33.   Since 1989 Usama Bin Laden has provided training camps and guest houses in Afghanistan, Pakistan, the Sudan, Somalia and Kenya for the use of Al Qaida and associated terrorist groups. We know from intelligence that there are currently at least a dozen camps across Afghanistan, of which at least four are used for training terrorists.

34.   Since 1989, Usama Bin Laden has established a series of businesses to provide income for Al Qaida, and to provide cover for the procurement of explosives, weapons and chemicals, and for the travel of Al Qaida operatives. The businesses have included a holding company known as 'Wadi Al Aqiq', a construction business known as 'Al Hijra', an agricultural business known as 'Al Themar Al Mubaraka', and investment companies known as 'Ladin International' and 'Taba Investments'.

Usama Bin Laden and previous attacks

35. In 1992 and 1993 Mohamed Atef travelled to Somalia on several occasions for the purpose of organising violence against United States and United Nations troops then stationed in Somalia. On each occasion he reported back to Usama Bin Laden, at his base in the Riyadh district of Khartoum.

36. In the spring of 1993 Atef, Saif al Adel, another senior member of Al Qaida, and other members began to provide military training to Somali tribes for the purpose of fighting the United Nations forces.

37. On 3 and 4 October 1993 operatives of Al Qaida participated in the attack on US military personnel serving in Somalia as part of the operation 'Restore Hope.' Eighteen US military personnel were killed in the attack.

38. From 1993 members of Al Qaida began to live in Nairobi and set up businesses there, including Asma Ltd, and Tanzanite King. They were regularly visited there by senior members of Al Qaida, in particular by Atef and Abu Ubadiah al Banshiri.

39. Beginning in the latter part of 1993, members of Al Qaida in Kenya began to discuss the possibility of attacking the US Embassy in Nairobi in retaliation for US participation in Operation Restore Hope in Somalia. Ali Mohamed, a US citizen and admitted member of Al Qaida, surveyed the US Embassy as a possible target for a terrorist attack. He took photographs and made sketches, which he presented to Usama Bin Laden while Bin Laden was in Sudan. He also admitted that he had trained terrorists for Al Qaida in Afghanistan in the early 1990s, and that those whom he trained included many involved in the East African bombings in August 1998.

40. In June or July 1998, two Al Qaida operatives, Fahid Mohammed Ali Msalam and Sheik Ahmed Salim Swedan, purchased a Toyota truck and made various alterations to the back of the truck.

41. In early August 1998, operatives of Al Qaida gathered in 43, New Runda Estates, Nairobi to execute the bombing of the US Embassy in Nairobi.

42. On 7 August 1998, Assam, a Saudi national and Al Qaida operative, drove the Toyota truck to the US embassy. There was a large bomb in the back of the truck.

43. Also in the truck was Mohamed Rashed Daoud Al 'Owali, another Saudi. He, by his own confession, was an Al Qaida operative, who from about 1996 had been trained in Al Qaida camps in Afghanistan in explosives, hijacking, kidnapping, assassination and intelligence techniques. With Usama Bin Laden's express permission, he fought alongside the Taleban in Afghanistan. He had met Usama Bin Laden personally in 1996 and asked for another 'mission.' Usama Bin Laden sent him to East Africa after extensive specialised training at camps in Afghanistan.

44. As the truck approached the Embassy, Al 'Owali got out and threw a stun grenade at a security guard. Assam drove the truck up to the rear of the embassy. He got out and then detonated the bomb, which demolished a multi-storey secretarial college and severely damaged the US embassy, and the Co-operative bank building. The bomb killed 213 people and injured 4500. Assam was killed in the explosion.

45. Al 'Owali expected the mission to end in his death. He had been willing to die for Al Qaida. But at the last minute he ran away from the bomb truck and survived. He had no money, passport or plan to escape after the mission, because he had expected to die.

46. After a few days, he called a telephone number in Yemen to have money transferred to him in Kenya. The number he rang in Yemen was contacted by Usama Bin

Laden's phone on the same day as Al 'Owali was arranging to get the money.

47. Another person arrested in connection with the Nairobi bombing was Mohamed Sadeek Odeh. He admitted to his involvement. He identified the principal participants in the bombing. He named three other persons, all of whom were Al Qaida or Egyptian Islamic Jihad members.

48. In Dar es Salaam the same day, at about the same time, operatives of Al Qaida detonated a bomb at the US embassy, killing 11 people. The Al Qaida operatives involved included Mustafa Mohamed Fadhil and Khaflan Khamis Mohamed. The bomb was carried in a Nissan Atlas truck, which Ahmed Khfaklan Ghailani and Sheikh Ahmed Salim Swedan, two Al Qaida operatives, had purchased in July 1998, in Dar es Salaam.

49. Khaflan Khamis Mohamed was arrested for the bombing. He admitted membership of Al Qaida, and implicated other members of Al Qaida in the bombing.

50. On 7 and 8 August 1998, two other members of Al Qaida disseminated claims of responsibility for the two bombings by sending faxes to media organisations in Paris, Doha in Qatar, and Dubai in the United Arab Emirates.

51. Additional evidence of the involvement of Al Qaida in the East African bombings came from a search conducted in London of several residences and businesses belonging to Al Qaida and Egyptian Islamic Jihad members. In those searches a number of documents were found including claims of responsibility for the East African bombings in the name of a fictitious group, 'the Islamic Army for the liberation of the Holy Places.'

52. Al 'Owali, the would-be suicide bomber, admitted he was told to make a videotape of himself using the name of the same fictitious group.

53. The faxed claims of responsibility were traced to a telephone number, which had been in contact with Usama Bin Laden's cell phone. The claims disseminated to the press were clearly written by someone familiar with the conspiracy. They stated that the bombings had been carried out by two Saudis in Kenya, and one Egyptian in Dar es Salaam. They were probably sent before the bombings had even taken place. They referred to two Saudis dying in the Nairobi attack. In fact, because Al 'Owali fled at the last minute, only one Saudi died.

54. On 22 December 1998 Usama Bin Laden was asked by Time magazine whether he was responsible for the August 1998 attacks. He replied:

> "The International Islamic Jihad Front for the jihad against the US and Israel has, by the grace of God, issued a crystal clear fatwa calling on the Islamic nation to carry on Jihad aimed at liberating the holy sites. The nation of Mohammed has responded to this appeal. If instigation for jihad against the Jews and the Americans . . . is considered to be a crime, then let history be a witness that I am a criminal. Our job is to instigate and, by the grace of God, we did that, and certain people responded to this instigation."

He was asked if he knew the attackers:

> ". . . those who risked their lives to earn the pleasure of God are real men. They managed to rid the Islamic nation of disgrace. We hold them in the highest esteem."

And what the US could expect of him:

> ". . . any thief or criminal who enters another country to steal should expect to be

exposed to murder at any time . . . The US knows that I have attacked it, by the grace of God, for more than ten years now . . . God knows that we have been pleased by the killing of American soldiers [in Somalia in 1993]. This was achieved by the grace of God and the efforts of the mujahideen . . . Hostility towards America is a religious duty and we hope to be rewarded for it by God. I am confident that Muslims will be able to end the legend of the so-called superpower that is America."

55.   In December 1999 a terrorist cell linked to Al Qaida was discovered trying to carry out attacks inside the United States. An Algerian, Ahmed Ressam, was stopped at the US-Canadian border and over 100 lbs of bomb making material was found in his car. Ressam admitted he was planning to set off a large bomb at Los Angeles International airport on New Year's Day. He said that he had received terrorist training at Al Qaida camps in Afghanistan and then been instructed to go abroad and kill US civilians and military personnel.

56.   On 3 January 2000, a group of Al Qaida members, and other terrorists who had trained in Al Qaida camps in Afghanistan, attempted to attack a US destroyer with a small boat loaded with explosives. Their boat sank, aborting the attack.

57.   On 12 October 2000, however, the USS Cole was struck by an explosive-laden boat while refuelling in Aden harbour. Seventeen crew were killed, and 40 injured.

58.   Several of the perpetrators of the Cole attack (mostly Yemenis and Saudis) were trained at Usama Bin Laden's camps in Afghanistan. Al 'Owali has identified the two commanders of the attack on the USS Cole as having participated in the planning and preparation for the East African embassy bombings.

59.   In the months before the September 11 attacks, propaganda videos were distributed throughout the Middle East and Muslim world by Al Qaida, in which Usama Bin Laden and others were shown encouraging Muslims to attack American and Jewish targets.

60.   Similar videos, extolling violence against the United States and other targets, were distributed before the East African embassy attacks in August 1998.

Usama Bin Laden and the 11 September attacks

61.   Nineteen men have been identified as the hijackers from the passenger lists of the four planes hijacked on 11 September 2001. At least three of them have already been positively identified as associates of Al Qaida. One has been identified as playing key roles in both the East African embassy attacks and the USS Cole attack. Investigations continue into the backgrounds of all the hijackers.

62.   From intelligence sources, the following facts have been established subsequent to 11 September; for intelligence reasons, the names of associates, though known, are not given.

   • In the run-up to 11 September, bin Laden was mounting a concerted propaganda campaign amongst like-minded groups of people – including videos and documentation – justifying attacks on Jewish and American targets; and claiming that those who died in the course of them were carrying out God's work.

   • We have learned, subsequent to 11 September, that Bin Laden himself asserted shortly before 11 September that he was preparing a major attack on America.

   • In August and early September close associates of Bin Laden were warned to return to Afghanistan from other parts of the world by 10 September.

• Immediately prior to 11 September some known associates of Bin Laden were naming the date for action as on or around 11 September.

• Since 11 September we have learned that one of Bin Laden's closest and most senior associates was responsible for the detailed planning of the attacks.

• There is evidence of a very specific nature relating to the guilt of Bin Laden and his associates that is too sensitive to release.

63. Usama Bin Laden remains in charge, and the mastermind, of Al Qaida. In Al Qaida, an operation on the scale of the 11 September attacks would have been approved by Usama Bin Laden himself.

64. The modus operandi of 11 September was entirely consistent with previous attacks. Al Qaida's record of atrocities is characterised by meticulous long term planning, a desire to inflict mass casualties, suicide bombers, and multiple simultaneous attacks.

65. The attacks of 11 September 2001 are entirely consistent with the scale and sophistication of the planning which went into the attacks on the East African Embassies and the USS Cole. No warnings were given for these three attacks, just as there was none on 11 September.

66. Al Qaida operatives, in evidence given in the East African Embassy bomb trials, have described how the group spends years preparing for an attack. They conduct repeated surveillance, patiently gather materials, and identify and vet operatives, who have the skills to participate in the attack and the willingness to die for their cause.

67. The operatives involved in the 11 September atrocities attended flight schools, used flight simulators to study the controls of larger aircraft and placed potential airports and routes under surveillance.

68. Al Qaida's attacks are characterised by total disregard for innocent lives, including Muslims. In an interview after the East African bombings, Usama Bin Laden insisted that the need to attack the United States excused the killing of other innocent civilians, Muslim and non-Muslim alike.

69. No other organisation has both the motivation and the capability to carry out attacks like those of the 11 September – only the Al Qaida network under Usama Bin Laden.

CONCLUSION

70. The attacks of the 11 September 2001 were planned and carried out by Al Qaida, an organisation whose head is Usama Bin Laden. That organisation has the will, and the resources, to execute further attacks of similar scale. Both the United States and its close allies are targets for such attacks. The attack could not have occurred without the alliance between the Taleban and Usama Bin Laden, which allowed Bin Laden to operate freely in Afghanistan, promoting, planning and executing terrorist activity.

Prime Minister Tony Blair's Statement Concerning Military Action Against Targets in Afghanistan

October 7, 2001

The full statement is set out below:

Tony Blair: As you will know from the announcement by President Bush military action against targets inside Afghanistan has begun. I can confirm that UK forces are engaged in this action. I want to pay tribute if I might right at the outset to Britain's armed forces. There is no greater strength for a British Prime Minister and the British nation at a time like this than to know that the forces we are calling upon are amongst the very best in the world.

They and their families are, of course, carrying an immense burden at this moment and will be feeling deep anxiety as will the British people. But we can take pride in their courage, their sense of duty and the esteem with which they're held throughout the world.

No country lightly commits forces to military action and the inevitable risks involved but we made it clear following the attacks upon the United States on September 11th that we would take part in action once it was clear who was responsible.

There is no doubt in my mind, nor in the mind of anyone who has been through all the available evidence, including intelligence material, that these attacks were carried out by the Al Qaida network masterminded by Usama bin Laden. Equally it is clear that his network is harboured and supported by the Taliban regime inside Afghanistan.

It is now almost a month since the atrocity occurred, it is more than two weeks since an ultimatum as delivered to the Taliban to yield up the terrorists or face the consequences. It is clear beyond doubt that they will not do this. They were given the choice of siding with justice or siding with terror and they chose to side with terror.

There are three parts all equally important to the operation of which we're engaged: military, diplomatic and humanitarian. The military action we are taking will be targeted against places we know to be involved in the operation of terror or against the military apparatus of the Taliban. This military plan has been put together mindful of our determination to do all we humanly can to avoid civilian casualties.

I cannot disclose, obviously, how long this action will last but we will act with reason and resolve. We have set the objectives to eradicate Osama bin Laden's network of terror and to take action against the Taliban regime that is sponsoring it. As to the precise British involvement I can confirm that last Wednesday the US Government made a specific request that a number of UK military assets be used in the operation which has now begun. And I gave authority for these assets to be deployed. They include the base at Diego Garcia, reconnaissance and flight support aircraftand missile firing submarines. Missile firing submarines are in use tonight. The air assets will be available for use in the coming days.

The United States are obviously providing the bulk of the force required in leading this operation. But this is an international effort as well as UK, France, Germany, Australia and Canada have also committed themselves to take part in the operation.

On the diplomatic and political front in the time I've been Prime Minister I cannot recall a situation that has commanded so quickly such a powerful coalition of support and not just from those countries directly involved in military action but from many others in all parts of the world. The coalition has, I believe, strengthened not weakened in the twenty six days since the atrocity occurred. And this is in no small measure due to the statesmanship of President Bush to whom I pay tribute tonight.

The world understands that whilst, of course, there are dangers in acting the dangers of inaction are far, far greater. The threat of further such outrages, the threat to our economies, the threat to the stability of the world.

On the humanitarian front we are assembling a coalition of support for refugees in and outside Afghanistan which is as vital as the military coalition. Even before September 11th four million Afghans were on the move. There are two million refugees in Pakistan and one and a half million in Iran. We have to act for humanitarian reasons to alleviate the appalling suffering of the Afghan people and deliver stability so that people from that region stay in that region. Britain, of course, is heavily involved in actually (indistinct) effort.

So we are taking action therefore on all those three fronts: military, diplomatic and humanitarian. I also want to say very directly to the British people why this matters so much directly to Britain. First let us not forget that the attacks of the September 11th represented the worst terrorist outrage against British citizens in our history. The murder of British citizens, whether it happens overseas or not, is an attack upon Britain. But even if no British citizen had died it would be right to act.

This atrocity was an attack on us all, on people of all faiths and people of none. We know the al-Qaeda network threaten Europe, including Britain, and, indeed, any nation throughout the world that does not share their fanatical views. So we have a direct interest in acting in our own self defence to protect British lives. It was also an attack (indistinct) just on lives but on livelihoods. We can see since the 11th of September how economic confidence has suffered with all that means for British jobs and British industry. Our prosperity and standard of living, therefore, require us to deal with this terrorist threat.

We act also because the al-Qaeda network and the Taliban regime are funded in large part on the drugs trade. Ninety per cent of all the heroin sold on British streets originates from Afghanistan. Stopping that trade is, again, directly in our interests.

I wish to say finally, as I've said many times before, that this is not a war with Islam. It angers me, as it angers the vast majority of Muslims, to hear bin Laden and his associates described as Islamic terrorists. They are terrorists pure and simple. Islam is a peaceful and tolerant religion and the acts of these people are wholly contrary to the teachings of the Koran.

These are difficult and testing times therefore for all of us. People are bound to be concerned about what the terrorists may seek to do in response. I should say there is at present no specific credible threat to the UK that we know of and that we have in place tried and tested contingency plans which are the best possible response to any further attempts at terror.

This, of course, is a moment of the utmost gravity for the world. None of the leaders involved in this action want war. None of our nations want it. We are a peaceful people. But we know that sometimes to safeguard peace we have to fight. Britain has learnt that lesson many times in our history. We only do it if the cause is just but this cause is just. The murder of almost seven thousand innocent people in America was an attack on our freedom, our way of life, an attack on civilised values the world over. We waited so that those responsible could be yielded up by those shielding them. That offer was refused, we have now no choice so we will act. And our determination in acting is total. We will not let up or rest until our objectives are met in full. Thank you.

Biography of British Prime Minister Tony Blair

Tony Blair, (1953-), prime minister of the United Kingdom (1997-). Born Anthony Charles Lynton Blair, he was educated at schools in Durham, England, and Edinburgh, Scotland. He then studied law at St. John's College in Oxford, England, before becoming a lawyer specializing in trade union and industrial law in 1976.Blair began his political career in 1983, when he was elected to Parliament as a member of the Labour Party. He quickly advanced to the party's front ranks during the Conservative administration of Prime Minister Margaret Thatcher (1979-1990), when Labour was the major opposition party. He was favored by Labour leaders Neil Kinnock and John Smith; they believed his more moderate positions would appeal to British voters, who, beginning in the 1979 general elections, had started to turn away from Labour and its pro-trade union policies. From 1984 to 1987 Blair was opposition spokesman on treasury and economic affairs. He then moved to various posts in the Departments of Trade and Industry (1987), Energy (1988-1989), and Employment (1989-1992). In 1992 he was promoted again, taking charge of domestic issues in the Labour Party's counterpart to the governing Conservatives' cabinet.After party leader John Smith died in May 1994, Blair was chosen to take his place. Almost immediately, Blair began working to make the party more mainstream, lessening its dependence on labor and trade unions and broadening the party's membership. In 1995 and 1996 the "New Labour" party, as Blair called it, rapidly gained in popularity, while at the same time a long economic recession and several scandals drastically reduced support for the Conservatives.This rise in popularity culminated in a landslide victory for Blair and the Labour Party in the May 1997 general elections. Labour had its best showing in

the history of the party, garnering almost 45 percent of the vote and coming away with 419 seats and a 179-seat majority in the 659-seat House of
Commons.Blair became the youngest prime minister in almost 200 years.
After taking office, Blair pledged to abide by federal spending limits and
programs established by the Conservatives. At the same time, he
launched ambitious new programs, calling for better relations with the
European Union (EU), separate parliaments for Scotland and Wales, and
reforms in welfare and health care.One of Blair's first accomplishments
as prime minister was to stimulate the faltering peace talks in Northern
Ireland. Soon after taking office he laid out a new timeline for the talks.
In October 1997 Blair met with Sinn Fein leader Gerry Adams, the first
time in 76 years a British prime minister had met with a Sinn Fein leader.
The peace talks were successfully concluded in April 1998, and referendums to approve the peace plan were voted on the following month in
Northern Ireland and Ireland.In his first year as prime minister, Blair
supported referendums that were passed in Scotland and Wales to
devolve powers from the British Parliament to a Scottish parliament and
a Welsh assembly. Blair and his party were highly criticized for a welfare
reform plan to cut benefits to single parents. However, they were praised
for a welfare-to-work program for jobless youths that placed many unem-
ployed in jobs. Blair was an important advisor to the royal family after the
death of Princess Diana in August 1997. The British people, grief-strick-
en by the tragedy of Diana's death, criticized the royal family for their
aloofness and lack of public presence. Blair helped convince Queen
Elizabeth II to hold a public funeral and to become a more visible symbol
to Britons.

Federal Response: Examples of Government Action Since September 11

Responding to the September 11 Terrorist Attacks

The President and members of Congress from both parties are implementing a $40 billion emergency response package to help deal with the tragic events of September 11. This funding will ensure that the U.S. has the resources to respond to and recover from the attacks and to protect national security.

Billions of dollars have already been released to assist in New York and the other impacted areas — and more funding is on the way. Examples of the important activities being funded in New York and the other areas include:

Federal Emergency Management Agency, $2 billion:
These funds will support overall emergency assistance in New York and other affected jurisdictions. This includes costs associated with debris removal and emergency protective measures, as well as individual and family assistance, search and rescue, and other disaster assistance efforts.

Department of Health and Human Services, $126.2 million:
These funds will provide assistance for the health-related needs of the disaster-affected areas of the New York metropolitan area, Virginia, Maryland, and the District of Columbia.

Small Business Administration, $100 million:
These funds will support $400 million in low-interest disaster loans for renters, homeowners, and businesses in designated disaster areas.

Department of the Treasury, $48.4 million:

These funds will support the immediate response and recovery needs of the approximately 1,000 Treasury employees who were located in or near the World Trade Center complex, most of whose offices were destroyed.

Department of Labor, $29 million:

These amounts will provide funding for: the Department of Labor's Dislocated Workers program to provide temporary jobs to assist in clean-up and restoration efforts in New York; assistance to cover immediate information technology and other costs of disaster recovery for unemployment insurance claims processing that need to be relocated; and the Occupational Safety and Health Administration's monitoring of health and safety at the disaster sites.

Department of the Interior, $3.1 million:

These amounts will provide funding for National Park Service and U.S. Park Police emergency response costs in New York City and Washington, DC, as well as increased security patrols in both cities.

Commodity Futures Trading Commission, $200,000:

The Commodity Futures Trading Commission's New York office, which was located in the World Trade Center, will use these funds to purchase computers and office equipment for its temporary space.

OTHER EXAMPLES OF FEDERAL RESPONSE ACTIVITIES

Federal Emergency Management Agency:

The President has authorized FEMA to provide an unprecedented level of assistance. For example, the President has authorized FEMA to pay for 100 percent of public assistance activities in New York and at the Pentagon (typically, states pay 25 percent of these costs). This marks the first time FEMA will cover the entire share of public assistance expenses. Examples of public assistance activities include debris removal and repair and restoration of public facilities. In addition:

- FEMA has assigned 11 Federal agencies to respond to the attack. Among the Federal agencies tasked to respond were the Department of Defense, Army Corps of Engineers, USDA Forest Service, Public Health Service, and EPA.
- FEMA has called up 10 FEMA Urban Search and Rescue task forces from around the Nation to assist in the efforts in New York and Virginia. Urban Search and Rescue task forces are teams of local emergency responders that have specialized FEMA training and equipment for rescuing people in the wake of disasters such as earthquakes and terrorist events.

Examples of additional FEMA action:
- The agency has also been working with local governments on the debris removal efforts.
- There are currently 3,571 Federal personnel, including 1,596 from FEMA, working in response to these incidents.
- Through September 27, FEMA had obligated $240.5 milion in New York and Virginia.
- FEMA has established Disaster Field Offices in New York City and Virginia where disaster victims may seeks assistance. FEMA also is operating a toll-free hotline for information and registering disaster victims.
- Through September 27, 115,756 tons of debris had been removed from the WTC site. The estimate for total debris at the WTC is 1.2 million tons.
- FEMA is helping city, state, and volunteer organizations organize a long-term strategy for using the millions of dollars in donated funds.
- Working with the American Red Cross and other volunteer and Federal agencies, FEMA has been providing humanitarian and financial assistance to disaster victims.

Department of Education:
- Provided $5 million for Rehabilitation Services Administration to help individuals who suffered disabling physical or mental trauma as a result of the WTC attacks, as well as funds to help previously disabled Americans who lost jobs, rehabilitation or other support struc-

tures as a result of the attack.

- Provided $4 million to New York City schools and $1.7 million to New York state schools for Project SERV grants that support counseling and mental health services for affected children.
- Department of Education also established a loan forgiveness program to help those who live or work in NY City by providing temporary relief from student loan payments.

Department of Labor

Labor is working to ensure the safety of the World Trade Center site for rescue personnel and is providing financial assistance to dislocated workers.

- Labor has also released $25 million of dislocated worker assistance to the State of New York to create temporary jobs to help with cleanup efforts.
- About 180 Occupational Safety & Health Administration (OSHA) staff have been deployed to provide around-the-clock safety and health assistance.

Department of Justice

- The President signed into law legislation that will speed payment of $152,000 in compensation to the family of each fallen police officer, firefighter and rescuer through the Public Safety Officers' Benefits program.
- The President also signed into law a victims compensation benefit program for expeditious payment of compensation to victims or their relatives for losses suffered as a result of the terrorist attacks. The program establishes a special claim process in the Department of Justice.

Health and Human Services (HHS)

- More than 570 (HHS) personnel are deployed in the New York City area to augment medical personnel assisting victims and recovery workers.
- HHS mental health services personnel and U.S. Public Health Service reservists are providing services to Federal responders and the public.
- The Centers for Disease Control and Prevention (CDC) has deployed personnel to assist the New York City Health Department in patient

care and follow-up needs.

- HHS has also made available about 100 doctors, nurses and other health care professionals to staff two treatment stations to provide round-the-clock medical care to rescue and recovery workers toiling in the aftermath of the attack in New York City.

Small Business Administration (SBA)

- Along with FEMA and other Federal agencies, SBA's Disaster Loan Program has set up Disaster Field Offices in New York and Virginia where disaster victims may come for assistance.
- SBA has sent out 5,677 applications for low-interest disaster loans. SBA has directly assisted 4,598 individuals and businesses with loan applications and other inquiries.
- SBA has already approved disaster loans totaling $6,052,900.
- SBA is also conducting information workshops at different locations around New York to reach as many disaster victims as possible.

Environmental Protection Agency (EPA)

- EPA is monitoring the disaster sites to ensure that rescue workers and the public are not facing dangerous environmental risks.
- Over 200 EPA personnel have participated in the response to the terrorist attacks in New York, Pennsylvania and Virginia.
- EPA has been responsible for cleaning and washing down of all workers, equipment, and resources employed during the rescue stage.
- The Agency is sampling air, water, and asbestos as well as conducting radiological and dust monitoring.
- EPA is also vacuuming and cleaning sidewalks, streets, and buildings in the World Trade Center area.

Army Corps of Engineers (Corps)

Corps structural engineering teams have been surveying buildings and structures in New York City so the city can assure the safety of search, rescue and debris-removal operations in and around the affected areas. The Corps is also developing a debris operations plan for the New York City. In addition, the Corps is considering potential improvements to a harbor facility for removing debris by barge.

Internal Revenue Service:

- The IRS and Treasury have extended deadlines for all taxpayers affected by the tragedy.
- IRS released new information to help the public use charitable organizations and has sped up the processing of requests for tax-exempt status from new charities formed to assist victims of the September 11 attacks.
- IRS created a special e-mail address for businesses to send their questions to the IRS and get answers about extensions and other relief stemming from the disasters.
- IRS issued a release reminding taxpayers who suffered property losses because of the September 11 terrorist attacks that they may get a quick tax refund by claiming these losses on an amended return for 2000.

American Liberty Partnership

Frequently Asked Questions

What is the American Liberty Project?

In a Rose Garden ceremony at the White House, President George W. Bush unveiled the American Liberty Project. The Internet initiative brings online support to those organizations that most need help — organizations that have been sustaining incredible burdens in order to serve the victims of the September 11 terrorist attacks and their families. Visitors can offer financial support to these organizations and obtain general information about the relief effort.

The partners in the American Liberty Project believe that the goodwill and resolve of the American people is more than equal to the task of meeting the needs that have emerged in these terrible days — and that will continue to emerge in the days and weeks ahead. The partners also believe in the power of the Internet to build communities around important causes and to provide critical support for nonprofit organizations.

How were the charities selected?

The charities highlighted on the American Liberty Project were selected in collaboration with the State of New York, City of New York, Office of the Governor of New York, the Commonwealth of Virginia, and the Virginia Emergency Response Team

Who are the partners of the American Liberty Project?

The partners include: Amazon.com, AOL Time Warner, Cisco Systems, eBay, Microsoft, and Yahoo!

How safe & secure is my donation?

The American Liberty Partnership does not use the personal information provided, except to complete the donation. In fact, personal information is disclosed to the charities only if you give us your permission. You may also choose to make your donation anonymously. The American Liberty Partnership will never sell, trade, or rent your personal information to other individuals or companies.

To keep online donations secure, the American Liberty Partnership uses industry-leading Secure Sockets Layer (SSL) technology.

How much of my donation will the charity receive?

Your contribution will go to your designated charity. The organization will owe no fees, charges or commissions on the contribution. The American Liberty Partnership is covering all of the transaction costs associated with collecting and distributing your contribution, including the fees charged by the credit card companies.

Is my donation tax deductible?

Yes. Donations made through the American Liberty Project Giving System are tax deductible. When you make a donation, be sure to save or print the confirmation e-mail you receive for your tax records. If you have any questions, however, as always, please consult a tax professional.

Who processes my donation?

The American Liberty Project is working in collaboration with PipeVine to process donations. PipeVine, also known as United Nonprofit Operations, Inc., is a public charity based in San Francisco, with a history of managing charitable payroll deductions and other contributions to nonprofit organizations.

Elementary School Letter

September 12, 2001

Dear Children:

Many Americans were injured or lost their lives in the recent national tragedy. All their friends and loved ones are feeling very sad, and you may be feeling sad, frightened, or confused, too.

I want to reassure you that many people - including your family, your teachers, and your school counselor - love and care about you and are looking out for your safety. You can talk with them and ask them questions. You can also write down your thoughts or draw a picture that shows how you are feeling and share that with the adults in your life.

When sad or frightening things happen, all of us have an opportunity to become better people by thinking about others. We can show them we care about them by saying so and by doing nice things for them. Helping others will make you feel better, too.

I want you to know how much I care about all of you. Be kind to each other, take care of each other, and show your love for each other.

With best wishes,

Laura Bush

United States Bill of Rights

Amendment I

Congress shall make no law respecting an establishment of religion, or prohibiting the free exercise thereof; or abridging the freedom of speech, or of the press; or the right of the people peaceably to assemble, and to petition the government for a redress of grievances.

Amendment II

A well regulated militia, being necessary to the security of a free state, the right of the people to keep and bear arms, shall not be infringed.

Amendment III

No soldier shall, in time of peace be quartered in any house, without the consent of the owner, nor in time of war, but in a manner to be prescribed by law.

Amendment IV

The right of the people to be secure in their persons, houses, papers, and effects, against unreasonable searches and seizures, shall not be violated, and no warrants shall issue, but upon probable cause, supported by oath or affirmation, and particularly describing the place to be searched, and the persons or things to be seized.

Amendment V

No person shall be held to answer for a capital, or otherwise infamous crime, unless on a presentment or indictment of a grand jury, except in cases arising in the land or naval forces, or in the militia, when in actual service in time of war or public danger; nor shall any person be subject for the same offense to be twice put in jeopardy of life or limb; nor shall be compelled in any criminal case to be a witness against himself, nor be deprived of life, liberty, or property, without due process of law; nor shall private property be taken for public use, without just compensation.

Amendment VI

In all criminal prosecutions, the accused shall enjoy the right to a speedy and public trial, by an impartial jury of the state and district wherein the crime shall have been committed, which district shall have been previously ascertained by law, and to be informed of the nature and cause of the accusation; to be confronted with the witnesses against him; to have compulsory process for obtaining witnesses in his favor, and to have the assistance of counsel for his defense.

Amendment VII

In suits at common law, where the value in controversy shall exceed twenty dollars, the right of trial by jury shall be preserved, and no fact tried by a jury, shall be otherwise reexamined in any court of the United States, than according to the rules of the common law.

Amendment VIII

Excessive bail shall not be required, nor excessive fines imposed, nor cruel and unusual punishments inflicted.

Amendment IX

The enumeration in the Constitution, of certain rights, shall not be construed to deny or disparage others retained by the people.

Amendment X

The powers not delegated to the United States by the Constitution, nor prohibited by it to the states, are reserved to the states respectively, or to the people.

I Pledge Allegiance
to the Flag
of the
United States of America
and to the
Republic for Which
It Stands;
One Nation, Under God, Indivisible,
With
Liberty and Justice
for All.

September 11, 2001